CATS : A Celebration

CATS : A Celebration

Elizabeth Hamilton
Illustrated by Ian Cox

Charles Scribner's Sons
NEW YORK

To
PRINCE
the black, golden-eyed cat
of
Kensington

1 3 5 7 9 11 13 15 17 19   I/C   20 18 16 14 12 10 8 6 4 2

Printed in Great Britain
Library of Congress Catalog Card Number 79-83681
SBN 0-684-16238-5

Contents

Acknowledgements

I would like to thank for invaluable advice Major W. S. H. Garforth, editor of *Cat*, the journal of the Cats' Protection League, and Mrs Nerea de Clifford, *ex officio* president.

For contributions and for consistent help and encouragement I owe a particular debt of gratitude to: the Rev Anselm ODC; Mr Richard Austin; Lord and Lady Barclay de Tolly; the Rev Sir Hugh Dacre Barrett-Lennard Bt Cong Orat; Mrs B. Bocking, hon secretary to *The Ark*; Mr Neville Braybrooke; Mr A. S. Bretell; Canon Reginald Cant, Chancellor, York Minster; the Very Rev Joseph Dessain, Canon Residentiary of Malines Cathedral; Mr and Mrs Duncan Jones; Mr John Ebdon, the Planetarium, London; Mr Sydney Farmer KSS; Mrs Marjorie Hunt; Capt and Mrs S. T. C. Luke and their daughter Lucretia; Mrs Koralie Hamilton Northen; Mr Reginald Racher, formerly verger of St Mary Abbots, Kensington; Mr David St John Thomas.

The many others to whom I am deeply grateful—some of whose names do not appear in the text—include: Miss Priscilla Balkwill and friends of hers at Lady Margaret Hall, Oxford; Mrs Phoebe Carter; Mrs Joan Chidson; Mrs Molly Cox, BBC producer; Miss Biddy Darlow; Mrs Susanna Edney; Miss Dorothy Fothergill; Miss Jackie Gazzi; Mr and Mrs B. M. Gorzkiewicz; Mrs Grace Hambling, formerly private secretary to Sir Winston Churchill; Miss Frances Head; the Rev Isidore ODC; Mr Ameer Janmohamed; Mrs Diane Kirby; Mrs R. Lada; the Rev Luke ODC; Miss Maeve Marsh; Mrs Isabel Melton; Miss Juliet O'Hea; the Rev Peter ODC; Mrs Ann Price; Miss Katie Price; Miss Annabel Redhead and Mr Brian Redhead; Miss Mary Scudamore; Miss Cathy Thomas; Mrs Truman and the late Mr Ralph Truman; Mr Neil Ware, Maggie Jones's Restaurant, Kensington.

Lastly, a word of thanks to the late Rt Rev Stanley Eley, Bishop of Gibraltar, formerly Vicar of St Mary Abbots, Kensington; also to the late Very Rev Dom Ambrose Agius OSB, editor of *The Ark*.

Acknowledgements are due to the following for permission to

use published material: to J. M. Dent & Sons Ltd, and the Trustees for the Copyrights of the late Dylan Thomas, for the lines from 'Do Not Go Gentle . . .' from the *Collected Poems* of Dylan Thomas; to Faber & Faber Ltd for the extracts from the *Collected Poems* of Louis MacNeice, *Archy's Life of Mehitabel* by Don Marquis, and 'Esther's Tomcat' from *Lupercal* by Ted Hughes; to the Melrose Press Ltd for the entry from the *International Who's Who in Poetry*; to the *New Statesman* for 'A Writer's Cat' by Neville Braybrooke; to Mr Hubert Nicolson for the lines from 'Cats', from the collection *Not Love Perhaps* by A. S. J. Tessimond; to *The Tablet* for 'Reflections in a Cat's Eyes' by Neville Braybrooke; and to Dr John Wall of the Medical Defence Union for his letter to *The Times*.

I also found a flood of information, anecdotes and comments in present and past numbers of *Cat*, the official bi-monthly journal of the Cats' Protection League.

Introduction

There are cats and cats, Diderot says. *Il y a chat et chat.*

Cats and cats. That is what this book is about. It is in the nature of a paean in honour of cats, an acknowledgement that cats can enrich our lives, and we, if we choose, the lives of cats. Indeed anyone who goes through the years indifferent to the beauty, the elegance, the ingenuity, the intelligence, the affection of which the cat is capable—such a person is as impoverished as one who, while walking along a country lane in summer, is blind to the flowers in the hedgerow, deaf to the song of birds, the hum of insects, the whisper of leaves in the wind.

A paean is a song of joy. But joy does not preclude sadness; a passing cloud can hide the sun, a child's laughter momentarily give place to tears. To encounter Arthur, the large white cat from the television advertisements, sitting on the counter of a laundry in Kensington—that was joy. To glimpse a lean, bedraggled stray scrabbling in a dustbin is sorrow, heartache.

There is, too, the sorrow that is a concomitant of the joy we derive from the companionship, even existence, of a treasured cat. You have only to read Dr A. L. Rowse's *Peter, the White Cat of Trenarren*. It is all there. The love uniting a scholar and poet to a 'little white shadow' of a cat; the pain, too, on both sides, occasioned by partings and prolonged absences; and, finally, the poignancy of death. 'For the life of a little cat', Dr Rowse writes, 'has its significance, just as the life of man—shares in the miracle of birth, the redeeming spirit of love, the mystery of death.'

This book is not a methodical, learned discourse. It is not written to instruct, but for pleasure—my own pleasure—yet in the hope that others, too, may possibly find in it something to please them. This is how it came about. One day there flashed into my mind the Biblical words: 'Let us now praise famous men.' 'Why not famous cats?' I thought. And not just famous cats, but cats as such: ordinary, commonplace cats who can be no less endearing than their patrician kinsfolk. And so this book was born.

8

It is an omnium gatherum of recollections, impressions, legends, anecdotes, both from my own experience and from that of friends and of members of the public who have sent me their stories. It is about cats I have known, cats in literature, ecclesiastical cats, services rendered by the cat, the language of the cat, the mystery of the cat and so on. The omission of all reference to witchcraft is deliberate. Plenty, I feel, has been written elsewhere on this morbid, horrific subject; I want my book to be joyful.

I

Cats I have known

Jemima, my first cat, was given to me by my parents when I was a child in Ireland.

It is a winter evening in County Wicklow. The large flagged kitchen with its whitewashed walls is lit by the glow of the fire visible between the bars of the range. In front of the range a little tabby on a wooden chair sits bolt upright, gazing into the fire. I stroke the top of her head, aware of the coat silky to the touch and, as my hand moves down her back, the ripple of muscles. Puss begins to purr. The only sound is the purring of the cat, the clink of a cinder, the ticking of the clock. 'Puss, puss,' I say, 'goodnight, puss. Goodnight, Jemima.' My feelings for Jemima were very much those of Lewis Carroll's Alice for her cat Dinah: 'A dear quiet thing . . . purring so much by the fire, licking her paws and washing her face . . . a nice soft thing to nurse.'

Although Jemima was my 'very own' I was not encouraged to take her to the nursery. 'The next thing', my mother used to say, 'will be the cat in your bed.' She had not forgotten a sister of hers, a spoilt child, who used to disturb the entire household with cries for her cat, Whitey. On mild nights, or when the moon was high, nothing would keep Whitey indoors. Equally, no amount of coaxing or scolding would quieten her mistress. In a high-pitched whine, punctuated by gulps, she would reiterate: 'I want Whitey, I want Whitey!' until sheer exhaustion sent her to sleep.

Jemima used to ask to be let out at night. In place of returning she had a habit of squeezing her way through what seemed an impossibly narrow opening in the roof of the greenhouse, then letting herself down on to a shelf crowded with geraniums, yet without causing damage to the plants. Sometimes, like the 'retired cat' of whom the poet Cowper wrote in his poem of that name, she was found in the morning curled up in a watering-can.

My mother was fond of Jemima. When kittens were expected she would line a box with newspapers and hay and place it in a secluded corner, Jemima superintending with apparent approval.

Sometimes, however, the cat had her own ideas. On one occasion when, despite the customary preparations, there was no trace of Jemima, my mother became anxious. Anxiety gave place to dismay when Jemima, with a litter of newly born kittens, was found in a drum-shaped leather hat-box which was a present from my father to my mother. Another time Jemima had her kittens in an abandoned rooks' nest in the chimney of a spare bedroom.

When there were visitors Jemima liked to sit among them on a tiger-skin rug in the drawing-room. Whereas in the kitchen her face had a dreamy, faraway look, in the drawing-room she came as near as a cat can to participating in the conversation. Alert, she would turn her head, looking now at one person, now at another, as if taking note of all that was said. Only when the vicar was among the guests did she behave differently. Why this was so—for he was an amiable man—we could not discover. On his entry into the room she would dart under the sofa and, crouching there, glower at him. Embarrassed by her habitual hostility, we used to endeavour, when the vicar was expected, to keep her out of the room. But with feline persistence she would find a way in—dart in, perhaps, behind the parlourmaid carrying the tea-tray or, slipping through an open window, land on the carpet with a plop. If the vicar made friendly overtures, she would stare at him with an expression that was nothing short of insolent, lift a paw as if to strike, then turn and disappear under the sofa.

On Christmas Eve Jemima joined the rest of us in the dining room at tea-time, when there used to be a little tree decorated with lighted candles, coloured balls and a silver star. She would sit close by, her eyes bright in the glow of the candles, reaching up a paw from time to time to pat one of the shining balls. Or she would walk round the tree, tail held high, pausing now and again to sniff the fragrant branches.

Beazer, a contemporary of Jemima, was a large-boned, bedraggled tabby, sullen-eyed, with a broad head, small ears that lay flat, and a thick tail that thrashed at the slightest provocation. He spent most of his time in the stables or the yard, or roaming a copse that reached away at the back of the yard. Once, in a stable, I saw him seated on the back of Paddy, a carthorse; but resenting, it seems, my intrusion, he jumped down and streaked past me through the open door. Occasionally from the kitchen you would see him crouching outside on the windowsill, his face plastered against the pane, eyes staring and hostile.

Jemima and Beazer were good mousers, but their territory differed. Beazer ranged the stables, barns and harness-room. Jemima was responsible for the interior of the house. She liked to sit motionless for hours on end in the pantry, her eyes fixed on a crevice in the wainscoting. Her one out-of-door duty was to see that my mother's White Wyandottes and Buff Orpingtons were safe from rodents. She would inspect the hen-house, then the 'run' in front of it, moving among the hens and chickens like a nurse among her charges. Her duty done, she would make her way out, leaping effortlessly on to one of the posts supporting the wire enclosing the run. Sometimes a rat dangled from her mouth.

Trevor, my brother, a tender-hearted little boy, thought it unfair that, whereas in general Jemima had the freedom of the house, Beazer was discouraged from coming in. One day he tried to pick up Beazer, intending to carry him into the kitchen. The cat lashed out. Blood streamed down my brother's cheek, falling in great splotches on to his white sailor suit. My mother, unnerved, exclaimed: 'Shoot that creature, someone, shoot him!' Trevor, who was devoted to the cat, shouted: 'Then shoot me too! I love Beazer.'

Beazer was not shot.

Some time afterwards, when Beazer was crouching under Paddy's manger, Trevor went into the stable and sat down in a corner, watching the cat from a distance. Presently Beazer came purposefully across the cobbled floor and, lowering his head, rubbed against Trevor's bare knees. After that, from time to time, he repeated his attentions. Otherwise he remained a 'loner'.

One winter's morning Beazer was found dead outside the stables. Trevor wept bitterly. He and I buried him with all solemnity— showing him a degree of honour in death that he had not known in life.

* * *

Desmond, a year or so younger than myself, lived a few miles from us. He too had a tabby, called Tiger, a fine cat with the four stripes on the top of his head that, according to tradition, are the mark of a 'holy' cat.

Tiger had his house in the garden, built of wood by Desmond and his brother. The ground floor served as a kind of barn where there was a plentiful supply of hay which provided bedding or carpeting for the floors above. The first of these was Tiger's bedroom. The next, which was his living-room, had a balcony, and jutting over this a flat roof which gave protection from the rain. A ramp led from the ground to the living-room. To go into his bedroom Tiger had to step aside off the ramp, but for an agile cat of his intelligence this presented no problem. On warm days Tiger would sit on the roof, sunning himself and looking down on the world below.

He was a placid, good-natured cat. When Desmond's mother gave a party, he allowed himself, without protest, to be taken, sitting up on the back seat of a wooden motor-car drawn by Desmond, and wearing a taffeta cloak hanging down behind and fastened under his chin with ribbon. His paws were ablaze with diamond rings bought at the Shilling Market in Dublin. 'Diamond rings on a cat! What nonsense!' said Desmond's mother. But Tiger took it all in good part.

* * *

My uncle's home in County Meath was overrun with cats, not because he wished it so ('One cat is worth twelve', he used to say), but because his daughter was infatuated with cats.

There were cats in the yard, cats in the garden, cats in the house. Tabbies, tortoiseshells, black cats and white cats, short-haired and long-haired. Cats lay curled on the sofa in the drawing-room. Cats sat on chairs in the dining-room or stood on their hind legs asking for titbits. Cats jumped on to beds, burrowed under eiderdowns. They mewed to be let in and mewed to be let out. They purred, miaowed, caterwauled, hissed, spat. A cat was liable to trip you up on the staircase or dash out of a corner and seize you by the ankle. I have, I confess, reservations about so many cats in one household. Cats *en masse* have a way of 'taking over'. Also, it is difficult to form a relationship with one among so many. You may think you have done so, when off he goes to join his feline companions. Cats in large numbers can seem all much alike. This is not so. Each remains an individual. You can be sure, however, that there will be a few 'boss cats' who domineer and chivvy the others.

I was not to see again so many cats together until years later in Rome, when looking down one night upon cats (perhaps forty to fifty of them) in Trajan's Forum. Silently—one at a time or in twos and threes—they emerged from among broken statues and columns washed to a milky pallor by the light of the moon, as though intent upon participating in some mysterious nocturnal ritual.

* * *

Old Tom Biddulph and his sister Caroline, cousins of my mother and devout members of the Church of Ireland, held family prayers each morning. We knelt on the dining-room floor, arms resting on the back of a chair—Tom, Caroline, visitors, cook, maids and, standing apart, head bowed, cap in hand, the gardener.

One morning Tom, his prayer book open in front of him, was booming:

'O ye whales . . . bless ye the Lord, praise him and magnify him for ever.'

'O ye fowls of the air . . .'

At that point a pair of cats began to yowl outside the window. Tom paused, glowered, then renewed prayers:

'O ye beasts and cattle . . .'

The yowls grew louder.

Again Tom paused. 'Can't someone stop those damned cats?' he boomed. Whereupon his sister, in a voice scarcely less powerful than his, retorted: 'They're not half as damned as you are!'

Prayers continued.

So did the yowling.

To Tom Biddulph I am indebted for my first awareness of the cat as belonging to a world wider than my own: the cat in history and tradition.

At Monasterboise in County Louth, he showed me a Celtic cross at the foot of which are carved two cats, one holding a kitten between her paws, the other a bird. Tapping one of the cats with his walking stick, he said: 'Puss, you see, is as old as time.'

He told me, too, how St Patrick drove snakes out of Ireland. It was no hardship for the saint, he explained, because he was helped by a long, thin, black cat, the arch-enemy of snakes, who, before the arrival of St Patrick in Ireland, used to sit on a silver chair in a cave at Clough, in Connaught, giving advice, in human language, to people who came from far and wide with their problems.

* * *

Cats peopled my childhood. True, I never saw my grandfather's cat, Great Tom, but I might well have done so, since I used to hear about him so much.

He was an extremely large, sedate, tabby, utterly devoted to my grandfather who, before sitting down to breakfast, used to pour out a saucer of cream-topped milk for Tom. It was a ritual, strictly observed. If anyone else attempted to give Tom his milk he stalked away in disgust.

When my grandfather died, Great Tom would neither eat nor drink nor respond to any efforts to console him. Hitherto strong and healthy, within a week he was found dead, stretched on the landing outside my grandfather's bedroom . . . And yet there are those who say that cats are incapable of affection for humans.

* * *

Our cat died.
Because this unbearably
Underlined for us
The transience of happiness, life,

You weeping
Dug his shallow grave;
I weeping
Laid him there,
Warm still.

(By mistake I caught sight of you afterwards,
Head in hands in the greenhouse.)

A stone is over him,
A forget-me-not plant at his head.

Proportion, please,
The nations are scarlet with pain
(Rhodesia, Vietnam, the Berlin Wall);
He was only a cat
But love anywhere is love,
And we are only human.

These unpretentious, moving lines I found typed on a sheet of paper on my table. I do not know who wrote them or how they came to be there. But, for me, they recall a very dear cat, Romulus, buried in our garden when we were living in England, in Buckinghamshire. My father buried him, I planted forget-me-nots on the grave.

Black, with a white parson's collar, white whiskers, white gloves and a white 'thimble' on his tail, he was a handsome cat. One of three belonging to an old gardener whose cottage was near our home, he took to coming in to us. First the garden, where he sat by a rosemary bush in the shade of an acacia tree. Then the kitchen. Then the drawing-room and, in it, the most comfortable chair.

One evening in May, he made straight for a vase containing narcissi, smelt them, then gripping one stem at a time in his mouth began to lift the flowers and lay them side by side on the table. Occasionally he glanced at us, as if to say: 'What a clever cat I am!' When we mildly rebuked him, he took affront, turned abruptly, sat with his back to us, tail hanging down, twitching. He liked to walk among the silver ornaments on the mantelpiece, patting this one or that, never knocking one over.

During his last and only illness he lay in his basket on a cushion wrapped in flannel, a small blanket spread loosely over him. Pitiably thin, he would only take a little warm milk or a sip of brandy given to him from a silver coffee spoon.

When Romulus died my father said: 'No more cats!' He could not face all over again this heartache.

However, the unexpected happened. In University College, London, a professor came up to me, carrying a cat-basket in his hand. He wanted a home for a Russian Blue. 'I thought Nicholas would help to console you', he said, 'for the loss of Romulus.'

Nicholas, with his thick, short coat and his amber eyes, was a delight to look upon. He was sensible, too, and intelligent. Having taken him home, not without misgivings, for fear he would not settle, I gave him freshly cooked flaked cod (his favourite dish, the professor had said), buttered his paws and drew his attention to a box I had lined with cushions and placed near the fire in the kitchen. He looked at the box, sniffed it, then looked around the kitchen as if making a general appraisal. Then he looked once more at the box and, twitching his tail, stepped into it with aplomb, and proceeded to wash. Lick. Lick. Lick. His ablutions completed, he made his bed, moving around in circles, lay down and slept.

Later, I took him into my father's study. He went from one object to another, examining each in turn. Table, desk, chairs, bookcases. For a moment he stood looking up at my father, then sprang on to his lap and began to purr, kneading with his paws. The ice had been broken, a bond of friendship forged.

* * *

'A professor came up to me, carrying a cat-basket in his hand. He wanted a home for a Russian Blue.'

Prince, a large elderly Manx cat, as dark as ebony, has the thick, short double coat characteristic of his species. The lack of a tail coupled with tall rounded hindquarters gives to him, as to others of his kind, a strange somewhat hoppity gait. Even so, he moves with dignity, at a fine pace. Or he sits in the garden in front of his home as motionless as a bronze cat from ancient Egypt, his golden eyes staring from out of the thick black fur as if into an immeasurable distance. Or, on chill, wintry days, he sits indoors on a window-ledge, between the curtains and the window-pane, his dark shape silhouetted against the curtains calling to mind one of Gwen John's feline drawings in the Tate Gallery.

Sometimes he crosses the road and sits on the steps of the Carmelite Priory, awaiting the coming in or going out of a particular monk whom he regards as a friend. One day this monk, while talking to Prince, glanced aside at a commonplace cat. He did not touch the cat or address a word to him, yet Prince, sensing that attention had momentarily been deflected from himself, hissed, spat, and then walked away. A little moody, perhaps, Prince is nevertheless, as Dr Johnson said of Hodge, 'a very fine cat indeed'. He lacks one thing only: a golden crown to rest upon his shapely head and match the gold of his eyes.

* * *

In the delicatessen there is a pair of cats, one the colour of marmalade, the other black. The marmalade cat is the more plump of the two, his coat thick and soft; the black one is lithe, and shiny as jet. Both are friendly, but the marmalade cat comes to greet you spontaneously. They are devoted to each other; when the black one disappeared for some days his companion was desolate, and he went around mewing disconsolately, tail drooping. Sometimes the two lie sardine-wise in a cardboard box, each enfolding the other in his paws. Or they take up separate positions on a shelf, sitting motionless, one in a space between tins of soup, the other between bags of sugar.

I have watched them go out together, then each proceed on his respective way, one turning left, the other right. The marmalade cat likes to walk a little distance, then sit for a while on the pavement watching the passers-by or gazing through the open door of a bookshop. The black cat makes a bee-line for a public house on the corner. He chooses licensing hours, and, as the doors are too heavy for him to open, waits for a customer to arrive, then slips in. He is on friendly terms with one of the barmen who gives him a piece of sandwich or a few potato crisps. He is a cunning cat: choosing an auspicious moment, when customers have dispersed, he jumps on to a table and makes the round, lapping up dregs in tankards and glasses, then slips away.

* * *

When the cat came to the restaurant in Kensington she was a small, nervous creature, her long tortoiseshell and white coat matted, her tail drooping, a scared look in her pale eyes.

As days, weeks, months went by, a transformation took place. Attention, affection, good food, left their mark. She is a big cat now, her fur soft as silk, her feathery tail held high or bent over so as to touch her back with the tip, her movements graceful. Her face, as pretty as a pansy, has an expression of serenity, and the lemon-yellow eyes, darkly rimmed, look out upon the world with self-assurance. She walks from table to table with a proprietary air.

Some of the clients she regards as her friends. She will spring lightly on to a lap uttering a soft mew or tapping a sleeve with her paw, indicating that a morsel of fish, chicken or meat would not be unwelcome. To others she is indifferent; they might as well not be there. As to those who are openly anti-cat, she sometimes deliberately makes her presence felt—sitting close to a table, staring up, as if determined to cause embarrassment. Occasionally she has been removed, but she usually finds her way back. Like royalty, she can be gracious, charming, or, if she chooses, haughty, disdainful.

One day she jumped on to a table at which I was sitting—a breach of propriety of which she is rarely guilty. Immediately her tail caught alight in a candle flame. I seized hold of it and put out the fire with my hands. Mistaking my intentions for unseemly familiarity, she leaped down in a huff and stalked away. A fortnight passed before I was forgiven.

The cat sits in the window or, on warm days, in the open doorway, watching pigeons or passers-by. To go outside would waken memories she would sooner forget of life as lived by a stray. The novelist Richard Austin, in his poem 'Restaurant Cat', written in her honour, evokes these shadows from the past flickering upon a reassuring, sunlit present:

Once the night was a vast
scavenger-cat, crawling through
the streets with cruel star-tipped claws,
so that you cowered in alleys, terror
an amber, flickering flame that leaped
in the darkness of your eyes. Then you slid
like a breath of wind into the sheltering
doorways, scratched for food beneath
the dustbin lids. Abandoned, derelict,
all you could do was howl to your companion,
the distant, urchin moon.

Now the smell of food is wafted
daily beneath appreciative whiskers.
Fat, sedate, almost imperious, you stalk
between the tables as haughty as a waiter
or a chef from France. The coat is dappled,
striped dark and fair, as though it glowed
beneath the sun. See how the fur is wrapped
around the body with such disdainful ease, watch
that pink-tipped yawn, given like a bored
society beauty who leaves a fashionable ball.

But you will never leave this place,
however much the sun invites you or the door
opens on a rush of air. You watch the street
beyond the window, and spread your body
in a patch of warmth. Now and again a small
tremor ripples against the flanks. Is it
a memory of those days of wandering, the nights
that stretched their star-lit claws?
Do I imagine, or is it an old fear I see now—
a flickering amber light in the secrecy of your eyes?

* * *

One evening I was asked if I would look at a tabby belonging to the Priory: he was unwell, it seemed.

Brought to me in one of the parlours and placed on the table, he toppled over on to his side and lay motionless. I lifted him, and, supporting him with my hands, examined him as best I could. His coat was in excellent condition, his nostrils cool, his eyes, when I could persuade him to open them, clear. After some deliberation it was decided that if in the morning he was not 'himself', the vet must be consulted. Meanwhile he was laid on a blanket in a box, protected from draughts.

In the morning he had completely recovered.

The mystery was solved only at a later date. After a festive occasion in the parish club, the cat was found going from table to table, lapping up the dregs in glasses.

A taste for alcohol is not uncommon among cats. Samuel Butler's friend, Miss Savage, wrote to him in 1879: 'My cat has taken to mulled port and rum punch, and is the better for it!' Jerome K. Jerome mentions a cat who continued to drink from the leaking tap of a beer cask until she collapsed in a stupor. Hilaire Belloc too knew beer-drinking cats, and P. G. Wodehouse tells a convincing story of the cat Webster who, having lapped up whisky spilt on the carpet, ran amok and attacked a padded stool. But Wodehouse was devoted to cats: he had seven in all, including the jet-black Poonah who would travel two and a half miles on his master's shoulder to fetch the post.

* * *

I was walking along a quiet road in Kensington one Easter Sunday morning when I saw two cats, coming from opposite directions, sit down facing each other in the middle of the road.

A third joined them. Having passed, I looked back. There were four now. I looked back again. There were five. They formed a circle—facing inwards, tails reaching out behind.

A coven of cats? A clowder of cats?

* * *

On an autumn day in Paris cats moved among the women selling chrysanthemums outside the cemetery of Père Lachaise. Inside, a lean black cat peered from behind first one gravestone, then another; then, darting on to the path, pounced on flame-bright withered chestnut leaves. A pair of tabbies lay sunning themselves on a mattress spread out to air in the window of one of the tall, quiet houses to the south-east of the cemetery that look down upon the tomb of Héloïse and Abelard.

In the rue de Vaugirard a cat deigned to greet me each morning with a gentle miaow, then rub against me, purring: a small, elegant cat, dainty in her movements, her thick blue-grey coat offset by a white bib and neat white gloves.

The rue de Vaugirard. It was this far, according to the account in *Histoire de mes Bêtes*, that the cat Mysouff used to accompany Alexandre Dumas each morning on his way from his home in the rue de l'Ouest to his office in the rue St Honoré. In the evening Mysouff was there again, waiting for his master in the middle of the road, where the rue de l'Ouest comes out into the rue de Vaugirard. That is, if Dumas was not late in returning, as sometimes happened. In the latter event Mysouff did not go in vain to meet his master. He did not go at all. His intuition (call it what you will) told him better. Madame Dumas, mother of Alexandre, would open the door to let the cat out. To no purpose. Mysouff was not interested: he continued to lie on his chair, 'curled up like a snake biting his tail'. Other evenings he left home at the customary time. If the door was closed he would scratch at it until it was opened. Seeing his master approaching, he would dash up to greet him, rub against his legs, then dance along the pavement ahead, looking back from time to time.

* * *

Where I was staying in Scotland a wall of the library was hung with the tails of wildcats. Each tail, solid as a rope, was tawny-grey, ringed with black—the black, blunt end not unlike a shaving brush. To think that so many cats had been destroyed to satisfy man's whim!

I roamed glens and bracken-covered slopes, hoping to see a wild-cat. Now and again I heard an eerie, blood-chilling call. Then, one

'I saw, a little way ahead, a large, broad "tabby-cat" face peering from out a clump of bracken.'

evening, when shafts of sunlight breaking from between thunder-black clouds accentuated each detail, I saw, a little way ahead, a large, broad 'tabby-cat' face peering from out a clump of bracken. The head was flat, the whiskers thick and drooping, the yellow-green eyes wide open. I stood stock-still. The cat stared at me. I stared at the cat. Then, in a flash, he turned and was gone. I glimpsed the heavy muscular body, the thick coat marked with black stripes and blotches, the rope-like tail.

Is this giant tabby, officially known as the European wildcat or *Felis silvestris*, the progenitor of the ordinary domestic cat? No, the progenitor of the domestic cat—so it is believed—is *Felis libyca*, the African wildcat, also called the Kaffir or Egyptian cat.

There are striking differences between the two breeds. Whereas *Felis silvestris* is a big-boned, heavily built tabby, *Felis libyca* is of a lighter, more slender build and has a long tail and a coat that is the colour of the desert, with here and there the merest shadow of a stripe.

There is a difference also of temperament. *Felis silvestris* is fierce, intractable. Even when brought up from kittenhood by human beings these cats revert to the wild state. Moreover, kittens born from a 'cross' between *Felis silvestris* and the domestic cat turn out to be no less savage than genuine wildcats. To what degree the ferocity of the European wildcat is innate, to what degree it is conditioned by man's relentless persecution, is questionable. Even the well-known, purring, affectionate Scrap, whose unique relationship with two human beings is movingly told by Ernest Dudley in his book of the same name, leaves a question-mark in that her 'patrons', in their goodness of heart, while enabling her to make contact with them if she chose, did return her to her wild state. I would like the book to have one more chapter!

Felis libyca, in contrast, is comparatively easy to tame. The earliest evidence of domestic cats comes from Egypt; Herodotus, the Greek historian and traveller of the fifth century BC, mentions Egyptian cats, and there are numerous tawny cats painted on Egyptian papyri and on the walls of tombs.

Gradually these Egyptian cats were introduced to the continent of Europe and to Britain, possibly by Phoenician sailors (Phoenicians came to Cornwall), and certainly by Romans: a cat was a necessity on board ship to keep rats at bay. According to a widely held theory, European wildcats, having interbred with these domesticated descendants of *Felis libyca*, passed on to the latter their tabby markings.

This seems reasonable, but it does not explain everything. Why, I would like to know, did an old villager in Norfolk, when showing me her two tabbies, speak of them as 'Cyprus' cats? I have been told that in the distant past seafarers from Cyprus, making what in those days were immense voyages, reached the East Anglian coast. But cats in Cyprus would, presumably, have come from Egypt, and would consequently be a pale tawny colour, not tabby. Yet John Aubrey records that Archbishop Laud, a great lover of cats, was given a present, in 1637 or 1638, of 'some Cyprus-catts, our Tabby-catts'.

And is it not odd that the European wildcat should take the name of his colouring from the East—that is, if the word 'tabby', as we are told, is derived from Attabiya, a quarter of Baghdad in which watered silk or taffeta was made? Yet another mystery of the cat. . . .

2

Glimpses down the centuries

In the temple of Bast

In ancient Egypt, in the desert to the east of the Nile delta, there was in a city called Bubastis a temple dedicated to Bast, the cat goddess, mistress of love and of matters feminine. So vividly does Herodotus, the Greek historian, describe this temple that you can see it all before your eyes, just as he saw it so many centuries ago. Made of red granite, its frontage adorned with carved figures no less than nine feet high, it stood on what was almost an island approached by two tree-shaded canals from the Nile, each a hundred feet wide, as well as by a paved road—it, too, bordered by trees so tall that they seemed to touch the sky.

Set in the very heart of the city at a lower level than the surrounding buildings, it was visible from every angle. Other temples, Herodotus says, might be larger or more costly to construct, but none was more pleasing to look at.

Within its sanctuary stood an immense statue of Bast.

In the British Museum a characteristic statue of this goddess shows her as a woman with the head of a cat. Large pricked-up ears taper to a point, the eyes are deep-set, the mouth wide and determined; a long nose gives to the face an expression of curiosity. She wears a close-fitting, short-sleeved garment with a V neck, reaching down to the ankles. In her right hand she holds a sistrum, a bronze or brass frame into which were loosely inserted three or four metal bars which jangled when the instrument was shaken. Sometimes metal rings were strung on the bars to increase the sound. In her left hand is a small aegis or shield surmounted by a cat, and at her feet sit four kittens.

An individual cat, if not actually identified with Bast—as is Paul Gallico's Thomasina—was nevertheless consecrated to the goddess. In the event of a fire it was considered more important to save cats than human beings. Moreover on one occasion, when an attack was launched by Persians who cunningly arrived carrying cats in their arms, the Egyptians could not retaliate for fear of injuring these sacred animals. Such veneration explains, among the finds of Egyptologists, the number of feline paintings, effigies, and carvings —not to mention mummified cats in thousands.

In paintings adorning tombs the cat appears again and again in a domestic context, as a pet, or sometimes, in hunting scenes, as a retriever. A faintly striped, sandy cat, his coral tongue protruding, his exceptionally long tail darkly ringed, sits under a cushioned chair . . . Another, whose lithe body, paling from orange to white, is bent almost into the shape of a hairpin, is devouring a fish held firmly in the grip of a forepaw . . . A tawny cat, among papyrus leaves, pounces upon a waterfowl struck down by her master's casting stick. It is quite modern and often amusing. After all, we are familiar with a cat's liking for sitting underneath something, whether a chair or table or a motor-car. We are familiar with the air of satisfaction with which a cat 'gets down' to eating a fish. As to the cat acting as a retriever, W. H. Hudson, the naturalist, mentions a cat who attached himself to some dogs to do precisely this. And I recall how, in Ireland, when my father went out of an evening to shoot a rabbit or snipe or wild duck, Jemima the tabby would often insist on accompanying him, sitting on his shoulder, then return on foot trailing a victim as big as herself.

Different in atmosphere are paintings on papyrus showing the Great Cat Ra—Bast, here, is identified with her father Ra, the Sun God—slaying Apep the serpent. In the background is the Persea Tree, the Tree of Life, for we are witnessing a conflict of cosmic proportions in which light is victorious over darkness, life over death. The victor is a deity, yet he is a cat. Fur on end, expression complacent, he uses a broad-bladed knife as he severs the serpent's neck with that nonchalant air characteristic to this day of the cat who is about to dispose of a snake.

The bond between divine and feline was close. Reflect in the British Museum on the cat who, towering aloft, dwarfs a shaven-headed priest kneeling before him. Or consider on the pillar in Turin the sons of Nebra making obeisance before a cat, and the accompanying inscription: 'The beautiful cat who endures, endures.'

Then there are the little cats: amulets in honour of Bast, ornaments to hang on necklaces and bracelets, or fashioned for the sheer joy of it: gold, silver, cornelian, green and blue porcelain. The cats assume all sorts of poses, indulge in all kinds of antics. Kittens cascade down their mother's back, peer from between her legs, sleep between her paws. A cat made of terracotta wears around his neck a cord from which hangs an inverted crescent, symbol of the moon with which the cat is associated. A wooden cat, a toy, has jaws that open and shut.

Specially imposing are the bronze cats, offerings in shrines and temples, sitting bolt upright, tails neatly folded around the legs, looking into space: inscrutable, aloof, enigmatic, awe-inspiring, mysterious. No two are identical. One wears golden earrings, another a necklace, a third a collar of lotus leaves, a fourth a crown formed from a coiled snake. A scarab beetle is embossed on the breast of another. Each is a cat, yet more than a cat: more, that is, than a household pet, a mouser, a hunter; more than a creature 'for the children, in the words of the eighteenth-century mystic and poet Christopher Smart, 'to learn benevolence upon'; more than a champion in a show, sitting in a cage festooned with rosettes, while crowds gape in admiration. Baudelaire understood:

> . . . chat mystérieux,
> Chat séraphique, chat étrange . . .

The solemnity with which Egyptian cats were buried bears witness to the reverence in which the animal was held. I do not know how many mummified cats were buried at Bubastis. And not only there: a countryman tilling the land at Beni Hassan came upon a feline cemetery where some 300,000 mummies were found, laid out on shelves.

A cat who had belonged to a humble home might merely be wrapped in a bundle, yet lovingly and respectfully. Those from wealthy households were embalmed with costly spices, then swathed in linen kept in place perhaps by intertwining ribbons, one red, one blue, or by plaited straw. The straw, as Champfleury, the nineteenth-century author of *Les Chats*, remarks, could give the appearance of a treasured bottle of vintage wine. The head, as a rule, was enclosed in a kind of papier-mâché helmet or mask covered with paint or gilded linen, the ears pricked, the whiskers made of golden wire. Sometimes a turquoise collar was worn.

A mummy found at Abydos, now in the British Museum, suggests, when seen from a distance, a demure Victorian maiden wearing a key-patterned bathwrap. I cannot but smile when I look at her. Yet the first time I saw a mummified cat the effect was very different. I was a schoolchild, one of a party being 'taken round'. I felt tears rush to my eyes. I wanted to get away, to be alone. At the sight of this wizened rag doll of a cat, a caricature of cats as I knew them, I was struck as never before by the transience of life, the actuality of death. 'Change and decay . . .' Then the kindly Egyptologist who was endeavouring to enlighten our ignorance began to tell us how sometimes mummified mice were buried with cats. I had to smile. There was something at once touching and amusing at this concern that, in the hereafter, cats should be provided with mice for their nourishment and diversion.

The mummies used to be placed in cases made of bronze or sandalwood or earthenware. Some of these cases are rectangular, perhaps with the figure of a cat on the lid. Others are moulded to the likeness of a particular cat, the eyes inlaid with crystal or obsidian. These latter cases open like an Easter egg into two halves, the line of demarcation extending up the chest, over the head, and down the back.

Arthur Weigall records a weird experience he had when he was excavating near Thebes in 1909. A case made of wood in the likeness of a black cat, with yellow eyes and yellow whiskers, had been left in his bedroom. Wakened in the night by what sounded like a report from a pistol he saw, in the moonlight, a grey cat leap across his knees, then dash through the window into the garden. Almost at the same moment he noticed that the two halves of the case had fallen apart and were rocking to a standstill, while between them sat a mummified cat, the bandages in which it was swathed ripped open at the neck. Looking out of the window Arthur Weigall saw in the garden not the grey cat but his own tabby, back arched, fur bristling, eyes glaring. He concludes: 'I will leave my reader to decide whether the grey cat was a malevolent spirit . . . which had burst its way through the bandages and woodwork and fled into the darkness or whether the torn embalming clothes represented the natural destructive work of time and the grey cat was a night wanderer which had strayed into my room.'

As to a cat's final destiny after death, there is no single explanation. Sometimes the tomb in which the mummy was placed was visualised as a kind of shelter or home, warm in winter, cool in summer, where provisions and offerings, placed there for the cat, were renewed by virtue of incantations offered by the priest at the burial.

But there were less materialistic concepts. According to one (associated with Osiris) a spirit, an Egyptian equivalent of the Greek Hermes, led the cat by her paw, guiding her on her way to paradise. The journey entailed mounting a ladder held in place by the gods who, if the cat was nervous, lifted her safely into a paradise that was a glorified Egypt with fish-ponds, vegetation, and opportunities to play and to hunt. For highly favoured cats there was a paradise among the stars. Possibly Goethe had this in mind when he visualised Muhammad's cat, Muezza, in the life hereafter, purring around his master. 'For holy', Goethe says, 'must be the cat whom the prophet caressed'—a reference to the story that Muhammad cut a strip off his robe rather than disturb his cat who lay asleep on it. To this day Muslims respect the cat. They allow cats into their mosques, whereas dogs are not admitted. I recall my pleasure in Jerusalem, in the great mosque known as the Dome of the Rock, at seeing a large amber-coloured cat walk in, tail held high, self-possessed, silent, and sedate.

Liberty and the law

It is recorded that the ancient Romans allowed cats, though not dogs, not only inside the temple of Hercules but into the *adytum* or inmost shrine. A down-to-earth people, they recognised the services rendered by cats in destroying rats and mice, not only in cities and on farms but in the granaries of their wide-flung empire.

But there was more than this in the Romans' attitude to the cat. They saw in the cat's independent ways a symbol of freedom.

In the temple dedicated to Liberty by Tiberius Gracchus, champion of the plebeians, the goddess is represented with a cat at her feet. Again it was as a symbol of freedom that the cat blazoned the standards of Roman legions. The *Ordines Augustei* displayed a green cat on a silver background; the *Felices Seniores*, the upper half of a cat, paw uplifted, on a red background; the *Alpini*, a cat with one ear and one eye.

Hence, down the centuries, the cat's place in heraldry. The crest of the Della Gatta family in Naples bears a cat couchant; that of the

German Katzen family, a silver cat on an azure field. Cervantes tells of the ever-victorious Timonel of Carceyona, Prince of New Biscay, whose shield displayed a golden cat as well as the word 'Miau' in honour of his lady Miaulina, daughter of Alfeniquen of the Algarve. And the crest of the Macpherson clan of Cluny is a wildcat.

Freedom, however, is possible only in the context of the law—is lived, indeed, with the support of the law. And the realistic Romans, while respecting the law in theory if not always in practice, realised the folly of making laws that cannot be enforced. For who—to revert to the cats in the temple of Hercules—can prevent a cat, once his mind is made up, from going where he chooses, doing what he chooses, even if it should cost him his life?

The independence of the cat and the impossibility of controlling his movements has been recognised to a considerable degree in later times. It is not without significance that St Ives, the patron saint of lawyers, is represented in the company of a cat.

When in 1865 an inhabitant of Fontainebleau set traps to ensnare cats who molested his garden, the owners of the cats brought the man to trial and won their case. The following points were made:

(a) The domestic cat, in view of the animal's utility to man in destroying rodents, should be protected by law.

(b) A cat, being to some degree, by his very nature, a wild animal, should be permitted to remain so, if he is to render the services expected from him.

(c) To put a cat under lock and key is impossible, if the creature is to obey the law of his own nature.

When, in a sheriff's court in Scotland, the plaintiff argued that a pigeon of his had been killed by a cat belonging to the defendant, the latter was acquitted. If, it was maintained, the defendant was at fault for allowing his cat to come into contact with the pigeon, the plaintiff was equally so in not having prevented the pigeon from coming within range of the cat. The owner of the cat, it was emphasised, was under no obligation to confine the animal to the house.

I was intrigued by a letter in *The Times* of 11 November 1975, written by John Wall of the Medical Defence Union:

A doctor briefed me as follows:

'One of my patients called to consult me at my surgery; the morning was extremely wet and blustery and, as he opened my front-garden gate, with his head down against the wind, my cat, which he had not noticed, fell from the top of the gate on to his head, knocking off his glasses (bi-focals), which were damaged and will require replacement . . .'

The patient thought the doctor should pay. Our Scottish legal advisers were consulted. No, they said, the doctor was not liable for the depredation, whether malicious or inadvertent, of his cat. Now, if it had been a dog . . .

The law, however, is not always on the side of the cat. A cat, unlike a dog, is not 'reportable'. A motorist who knocks down a cat is not obliged, as the law stands, to report what has happened to the police or anyone else: he can pitch the animal into, say, a field and drive on, leaving the owner to search in helpless misery.

Felis britannicus

In Britain, as elsewhere, the Romans relied on cats to protect their granaries from rodents.

During excavations in 1949 at Lullingstone in Kent there were found the remains of a domestic cat killed by falling masonry. It is strangely moving, too, to see the marks of a cat's paws outlined on cement walked on before it had dried.

From Roman times the domestic cat became more and more part of the scene; nor does he appear to have differed greatly from the household cat we know today. He should be 'perfect of claw', said Howel the Good, King of Wales, who died in AD 948. This was essential if he was to be a good mouser. So were good hearing and sight. And there should be no scorch marks on his coat—caused, presumably, by sparks from a wood fire when the cat lay too close to the hearth. We are all familiar with the cat's passion for warmth, whether it be from a log fire, a coal fire, a radiator, an airing cupboard, a hot-water cistern or even an electric stove. I recall finding a cat of mine, while lunch was being cooked, sitting, paws tucked under him, alongside a steaming saucepan; and a cat who suffered from rheumatism in his tail used to sit in an alcove alongside the kitchen range, his tail immersed in a copper of hot water.

An Englishman, Friar Bartholomew, in his book *On the Nature of Things*, wrote rather charmingly in the thirteenth century: 'Some catte is white, some red, some black, some skewed and speckled . . . He is led by a straw and playeth therewith. And he is a right heavy beast in age and full sleepy and lyeth slily in wait for mice.'

An English bestiary of the same period shows two cats: one is busy washing himself, a hind leg jutting into the air; the other stands on his back legs, a mouse between his paws. Underneath, in Latin, are the words: 'He is called a mouser (*musio*) because he is a menace to mice.'

Another bestiary shows a couple of sprightly black cats coming along at a fine pace, one behind the other. The tail of the first is held erect, that of the second horizontally. A third cat comes up in the rear.

Because the cat was useful and quiet he was the one animal permitted in a convent. The English Nuns' Rule, dated 1205, includes the words: 'Dear Sisters, you must keep no beast other than a cat.'

In the Chester Miracle Play the cat is not forgotten. Mrs Hamm and Mrs Jaffett, when the animals begin to process into the Ark, say: 'Heare cattes, make carousal.' Whereupon the cats join in: 'Kyrie eleison.'

Chaucer understood better than some people of our own day that if you want a cat to kill mice you must feed him properly to build up his energy. He understood, too, the cat's love of comfort and his fastidiousness. What he says (much of it is in the *Manciple's Tale*) amounts to this. Give your cat plenty of milk. Give him plenty of meat—tender meat, not any old scraggy bit. Provide him with a comfortable place to sleep (he suggests a cushion of silk). Play your part, and he will play his. At the first glimpse of a mouse he will be after it, all dainties and luxury forgotten.

As to Dick Whittington's cat, doubt has been cast on his existence. But to most people the 'demythologising' of this famous cat is unacceptable. Two sixteenth-century portraits, one of them in the Mercers' Hall in London, show Whittington in the company of his cat. There is, too, the lordly white cat looking down, with his master, from a window in Westminster Abbey; and the rather splendid stone cat gazing upon the world from the top of Highgate Hill.

In Tudor times it was said of Sir Henry Wyat of Allington Castle that he used 'ever to make much of a cat'. When imprisoned he was visited not once but many times by his cat who, the story goes, would bring him a pigeon subsequently cooked by the gaoler.

Similarly consoled when in prison was Henry Wriothesley, Third Earl of Southampton. According to one version his wife, when visiting him, brought the cat with her. Others say that the cat came on his own initiative, making his way down the chimney. Two paintings show a handsome black cat with a white front in the company of his master. In one he supports between his paws a book emblazoned with the Earl's coat-of-arms.

In Holyrood House, Edinburgh, there is a panel said to have been embroidered by Mary Queen of Scots when she was a prisoner under the custody of the Earl and Countess of Shrewsbury. An

'When imprisoned he was visited ... many times by his cat who ... would bring him a pigeon subsequently cooked by the gaoler.'

ample, formidable cat with clearly defined eyebrows and whiskers, her long nose giving to her an expression of cunning, looks fixedly at a solitary mouse. A trace of what appears to be a golden crown on her head suggests the possibility that cat and mouse symbolise Queen Elizabeth I and the ill-starred Mary Stuart.

The continent of Asia

As in Egypt, so in Asia the cat has been particularly revered. A Sanskrit manuscript going back to 1000 BC mentions cats, and there are stories about them in the Indian epics which belong roughly to 5000 BC. The Indians, a quiet-loving people, were understandably attracted to this gentle, graceful and usually silent creature. A Hindu household was required to feed at least one cat. There was a law, too, that anyone who killed a cat must retire into the forest and, until he had made reparation, dedicate his life to the service of the animals.

The Chinese, a nation of thinkers and philosophers, admired the cat's capacity to sit motionless for hours on end as though deep in thought.

Chu Hou-Tsung, Emperor of China in the sixteenth century, had a cat with a faintly blue coat and jade-white eyebrows. Her name, Shuang-Mei, meant 'frost-eyebrows'. She was continually in attendance on her master, leading the way wherever he went, and when he was asleep she lay close by, still as a log. At her death she was given an exceptionally grand funeral in the mountains.

Established in China by the fifth century AD, elegant white cats with tawny markings, called 'lion cats', were kept as pets. There were others less elegant but highly valued for their services to man. Tama, meaning 'jewel', was a name often given to a cat.

Cats employed to protect silkworms from rodents were in such demand that sometimes there were not enough available, in which case farmers, as a last resort, displayed likenesses—pictures or carvings—representing the 'silkworm cat'. After the harvest was brought in, sacrifice used to be offered to the cats as a reward for having killed rats and mice who otherwise would have destroyed the crops.

Cats, however, could behave—according to Chinese tradition—in a disconcerting manner. This included walking on their hind legs, talking in human language, and producing dancing balls of fire.

The Empress Wu Chao (AD 624-705) went as far as to banish cats from her palace. This was because a lady-in-waiting whom she had commanded to be put to death threatened that in the after-life she would turn the Empress into a rat, and herself, in the form of a spectre cat, hunt her.

Cats' eyes, it was believed, changed to match the pattern of the sun, the pupil narrowing progressively until at midday it was as thin as a hair, after which it proceeded to dilate again. Hence the Chinese custom of telling the time by looking at the eyes of a cat. Baudelaire tells of two missionaries travelling in China who asked a boy whether it was yet noon. Hesitating a moment the boy went away and returned carrying a large cat. Raising with his fingers the eyelids of the animal he said: 'It's not noon yet'—which proved to be true. One of the missionaries in recounting the story added that the cat, though obviously none too pleased, behaved with 'exemplary forbearance'.

The Chinese, observing the sensitivity of cats to a change of atmosphere, believed that the animals could foretell rain. One cat, who slept on a bed of peonies, was reputed to wink when rain was on the way.

This belief, however, was not confined to China. In England, before the fens were drained, every household kept a cat to give warning of floods, which the animal did by going upstairs and settling on the highest shelf, cupboard or beam. On Sundays, as a mark of appreciation, the owners of the cats took them to church, and afterwards for a stroll which was known as the 'cats' walk'. Moreover, in 'A Description of a City Shower' Jonathan Swift writes that, when rain is approaching,

> the pensive Cat gives o'er
> Her Frolics, and pursues her tail no more.

From China the cat was introduced in about the tenth century into Japan, where he was called 'the tiger who eats out of the hand'.

The Emperor Ichigo (AD 986-1011) was particularly devoted to cats. When, on the nineteenth day of the ninth month of the year 999, kittens were born in the palace, royal attendants were allotted the task of serving them tasty dishes and even, in some instances, providing them with clothes. The Emperor conferred the rank of fifth lady of the court upon one of the palace cats, giving to her the name Myobo no Omoto, meaning lady-in-waiting.

Sacrifices were made to a cat known as the Guardian of the Manuscripts, whose responsibility was to protect papyrus rolls from the incursions of rats and mice.

Japanese fishermen used to take on board a cat, not simply to keep the boat free of rodents, but to protect the crew from ghostly visitants who, it was said, were disposed to appear at daybreak and twilight. But there are many tales too of spectre cats: one traveller who, making his way over the mountains, decided to pass the night in a ruined temple, was wakened by a bevy of such phantoms dancing and caterwauling.

An attractive exhibit in the British Museum is what is called a 'beckoning cat', about six and a half inches high, carved out of pearwood, her paw raised in a gesture of invitation, a kitten seated on her head. Cats of this kind used to be displayed outside shops to attract customers.

In Tokyo the Go-To-Ku-Ji temple, built not much more than two hundred years ago, is decorated with picture after picture of the Maneki-Neko cat, better known as the Japanese Bobtail, each one holding up a paw in greeting. A photograph of what was probably the first of this species to be seen in England was taken in 1910 by Dr Lilian Veley and published in *Cat Gossip*. It shows a comfortable looking white cat with a black mask, a broad, black, roughly triangular tail and, on her back, a large black patch shaped like a kimono—hence the popular name Kimono Cat. Dr Veley explained that these cats were said to contain the soul of an ancestor and for that reason were privileged to inhabit a temple.

In the feline cemetery adjoining the Go-To-Ku-Ji temple is an imposing carving of the 'Spirit Cat' who presides over the many cats buried there. Not the least spirit-like in appearance, solid, plump, his wide-open eyes on the alert, he sits up wearing a collar and a medallion.

In contrast, delicacy of line, detail and colour characterises the work of Japanese painters of both the past and the present. One of my favourites among the moderns is Tsuguharu Foujita, who died some ten years ago: though working in Paris, he remained true to the traditions of his forebears. One painting on silk that I find particularly delightful shows a cat peering from behind a screen, whiskers bushy, a red and green scarf draped about his neck, gazing wide-eyed at a spider. In another, a cat, while washing his face, stares mysteriously at his reflection in a bowl of water. A third shows plump kittens, one white, one white splotched with black, playing among flowers—the faces of the kittens as pretty as the freshly opened blossoms.

In Japanese prints cats often appear in the company of elegant pensive ladies wearing trailing kimonos, their hair piled high. The charming skewbald and piebald cats are as decorative as the birds, the butterflies, the almond blossom, the water-lilies, that make up their world. Further, these cats are amusing. They have a sense of humour. They spring surprises on their mistress—tugging at the hem of her kimono, chewing a blossom—or, when a princess is being wooed, suddenly dart away, helter-skelter out of the royal presence.

To generalise for a moment, all too often in paintings a cat is a mere accessory, an added decoration and, even though the artist is talented, badly portrayed. In contrast, the Japanese cats are alive. There is a striking rapport between the kimono-clad ladies and their pets. The bond uniting human and feline is as strong, for instance, as in Renoir's *L'Enfant au chat*, where the girl and the cat on her lap are alike serene and relaxed. This is even more striking in his *Le Garçon au chat*: a dreamy languor permeates the two. The boy's cheek rests against the cat's head, his arms enfold the cat, her tail is coiled upon his wrist. A similar rapport between human and cat is conveyed in Boris Anisfeld's portrait of his daughter, Morella Borisnova. The little girls's black hair is matched by the black fur on the upper part of the cat's head, her pale face by his white face, pale arms by white paws: a delicate pale hand caresses a black feline brow.

Even in pictures where the relationship is less intimate, the presence of a cat can give life, warmth—fill what could have been a void. Look at David Hockney's *Mr and Mrs Clark and Percy*. Hide from view for a moment Percy, the sedate white cat sitting upright on Mr Clark's lap . . . the nucleus, the core of the picture, has gone.

3
The writer and his cat

The cat has been the friend, indeed the solace, of many writers. Imaginative, creative persons, who feel the need of solitude as distinct from isolation, find in the cat an ideal companion. As early as the ninth century, an Irish monk at the Abbey of St Paul at Reichenau, Carinithia, wrote of his relationship with his white cat Pangur Bán: each busy, one with his studies, one with catching mice, neither interfered with the other, yet each provided company which was much appreciated.

Highly sensitive (no animal is more easily affronted), the cat in general is discreet, dignified, affectionate, quiet. He is also mysterious, a trait which works upon and fires the imagination.

True, he can be a nuisance. Edmund Blunden, writing in 1964 to Neville Braybrooke, complained of paw-marks left on his study table, but I don't think this was meant to be taken very seriously. With a few exceptions—such as Pierre de Ronsard, who feared and disliked cats, yet wrote of them superbly—writers have welcomed the proximity of feline companions.

If, for this reason or that, ideas will not take shape, words will not flow, I would suggest—to dislodge the blockage, to release the tension—not pep-pills or tranquillisers. No, I would suggest looking into the eyes of a cat. In speculating upon the mystery of pupils now dilating, now contracting, the mystery of a gaze that outdistances my own, sees things that I do not see, I feel steal over me a strange contentment, a serenity, an acceptance of lesser mysteries lost in a single, all-embracing mystery, even as specks of light are lost in the over-all brilliance of the sun.

The writer and critic **Neville Braybrooke**, one of whose earliest memories is of his father holding up a tabby cat at the bars of his cot, has summed up this feeling in his poem 'Reflections in a Cat's Eyes' about his own cat Fooff:

> Half a life I have spent with cats, or a cat, on my desk
> I am not a much travelled man

Malta is the farthest south I have been
I remember the pumpkins growing wild by the road's edge

Yet if I stare into the face of my 15-year-old cat
I do not regret the lack of journeys
For when I look into his contracting, dilating pupils
I travel in depth

Sometimes at night when I switch on the lamp
His eyes burn red in the glare
But when the morning breaks
The day fans these embers into sapphire blue flames.

The afternoons remain more philosophical
Between tea and supper—
Across a desk strewn with papers—
Our eyes meet, blur and reach the infinite.

James Boswell, despite an antipathy to cats, has immortalised **Samuel Johnson's** Hodge, who for years kept his master company in his rooms in Fleet Street.

He recalls how the cat would happily scramble up Dr Johnson's chest, while the Doctor, smiling and whistling, stroked Hodge's back and pulled his tail. When Boswell, feeling called upon one day to make some comment, remarked that Hodge was certainly 'a fine cat', Dr Johnson replied that he had, in the past, possessed even finer cats. Then, fearing that Hodge, hearing this, might be out of countenance, he added: 'But he is a very fine cat, a very fine cat indeed!'

Another time, when talking about a young man who went around shooting cats, Dr Johnson, as if in a reverie, said: 'Hodge shall not be shot. No. No. Hodge shall not be shot!'

Such was the Doctor's devotion to the cat that he used to go out himself to buy oysters for him. He feared that the servants, if asked to do so, might resent being put to the trouble, and so 'take it out' on poor Hodge!

'Dickens himself was attached to a white cat, William . . .'

Remarking on the absence of animals in Thackeray's *Vanity Fair*, George Moore recalls, in contrast, the cats in the novels of **Charles Dickens,** where they contribute in turn to the realism, the humour and the melodrama of the work. In *Dombey and Son* Mrs Pipchin's elderly cat, little Paul Dombey's companion, purrs contentedly, curled in the fender, the contracting pupils of his eyes looking like 'two notes of admiration'. In *Bleak House* there is the cat belonging to Vohles the lawyer; the Jellybys' cat who surreptitiously laps up Mrs Jellyby's milk; and Mr Krook's cat, the sinister Lady Jane, who follows her master and sits on his shoulder, hissing. When Lady Dedlock's lover dies the doctor shoos the cat out of the room —possibly a 'left-over' from the superstition that if a cat were to jump over a corpse the soul of the deceased would enter the cat. In *The Pickwick Papers* cats are the victims of a maker of pies.

Dickens himself was attached to a white cat, William, whose name, when kittens were born, had to be changed to Williamina. To accommodate her kittens, Williamina chose a corner in the writer's study and carried them there, one by one, from the kitchen. None too pleased, Dickens ordered them to be removed. In vain. Williamina persisted, and finally put the kittens not in the corner but at the feet of her master. This time they were allowed to stay, and as they grew bigger they thoroughly enjoyed themselves, scampering behind bookcases, swarming up curtains, playing on the table at which Dickens wrote. Homes were found for all except one, who came to be known as The Master's Cat, so devoted was she to Dickens. She liked plenty of attention. One night, while Dickens was reading, the candle went out. He lit it, stroked the cat and continued to read. Presently the light flickered. Dickens glanced up. He saw The Master's Cat snuffing the wick with her paw, then looking at him appealingly. The hint was not ignored. The Master fondled his cat.

Charles Waterton, naturalist and scholar, heartbroken at the death of his girl-wife, devoted himself to the study of nature, particularly animal and plant life, at Walton Hall, near Wakefield. Specially concerned for the welfare of his cats, he had a 'snug little box' placed against the wall where they would be warm in winter and in summer protected from the heat.

Out-of-door, stable-yard cats are, all too often, left to fend for themselves, on the assumption that the less food they are given the more eagerly they will hunt rodents. The truth, as Pasteur pointed out, is otherwise: if they are not fed adequately they have not the stamina to be good mousers.

Waterton gave his cats one large meal a day, consisting of raw fish caught in the lake. He fed them himself, talking to them affectionately as he did so. He was careful to see that fish bones were thoroughly crushed with a hammer so that they could be swallowed without causing damage. The cats were also given lavish and frequent helpings of milk fresh from the cow.

All this took place in a saddle-room made over to the cats. A window was permanently open so that they could come and go at will. Appreciating that cats like warmth, Waterton had a fire in an open hearth burning there at all hours.

Disliking the smell of tobacco, he would allow no smoking in Walton Hall. One day a couple of guests sneaked out of doors to enjoy their cigars in the retirement of the saddle-room. Waterton gave them short shrift. He saw no reason, he said, why the cats should be put off their food by the stink of tobacco. A notice to this effect was plastered on the door.

One of **Théophile Gautier's** cats used to watch the movement of his master's pen, nodding his head at the beginning of each line.

A strange character, Gautier has to be seen against the background of the Romantic age with its eccentricities. There was greater depth in him than might appear. His study of cats led him to the conclusion that the cat is methodical, philosophical, given to silence, tenacious of his own will; an ideal companion in solitude, melancholy and toil. For a whole evening he will, if so disposed, remain on your knee, purring, happy to enjoy your company. Put him down and back he jumps with a cooing note of gentle reproach. Or he will sit on the carpet, looking up, his eyes so full of tenderness that it is hard to believe there is not a soul there.

Gautier's affection for his cats went deep, whether it was the elderly animal who, when an argument broke out between the then young Théophile and his mother, nipped Madame Gautier's leg, to show where his sympathy lay; or his spoilt pedigree darlings, dynasties of cats 'as numerous as the Pharaohs of Egypt'.

To Madame-Théophile—an elegant 'red' cat with a white breast, pink nose, and blue eyes—he had given his own Christian name, so close, he felt, was the bond between them. She slept on the end of his bed, sat on the arm of his chair, delighted in exotic scents, especially patchouli and the perfumes exhaled by Indian shawls. Normally self-possessed, she was disconcerted on the appearance of a green parrot which Gautier was looking after for a friend; she seemed to think that the bird was some kind of chicken. Then, when it spoke in human language, she was terror-struck and hid under the bed.

Gautier's cats had impressive names. There was Childebrand, a splendid tiger-like animal, tawny brown striped with velvety black, his almond-shaped eyes a clear green. A kitten from Havana, 'white as a powder-puff', appropriately named Pierro, became in maturity Don-Pierro-de-Navarre. This cat, as soon as he saw a book lying open, would turn over the pages with his paw. He would try, also, to take the pen out of his master's hand. He insisted on going to bed punctually and preceded Gautier up the stairs like a page. He slept on the bed-rail, balancing as though he were a bird on a branch.

Three black kittens, born when everyone was talking about Victor Hugo's *Les Misérables*, were named Enjolras, Gavroche and Eponine. There was no difficulty in distinguishing the three little faces, each as 'black as a harlequin's mask'. Enjolras, who had a broad, lion-like head, full whiskers, and a feathery tail, was 'theatrical'. Gavroche indulged in comic tumbles, twists and twirls. Eponine, more elegant than her brothers, was highly nervous and warmly attached to her master. She would escort visitors from the hall door to the salon, keeping up, as she did so, a conversation composed of gentle murmurs and miaows. During meals she sat on a chair at Gautier's side, showing, throughout, a propriety that would have put many children to shame.

Foss, **Edward Lear's** big striped cat, who had a thick tail no more than a few inches long, lived to be seventeen, dying in 1888 a few months before Lear himself. During all this time he was his master's constant companion, making up in some degree for Lear's disappointment in human relationships. An old rip, Foss is immortalised in a series of pen drawings done by Lear to give pleasure to a little girl. Each bears a label, for example *Foss Rampant*, *Foss Couchant*, *Foss Dansant*, and so on. After completing seven of these Lear ceased: it was a shame, he said, to caricature his dear, faithful friend. Nevertheless, Foss appears repeatedly in the margins of Lear's letters.

At San Remo Mr Lear decided to build a new villa because his view over the sea had been spoilt by the construction of a hotel. He planned this villa to resemble the previous one in every detail, for fear that, if things were different, Foss might not approve.

To Edward Lear we are indebted not only for Foss but for the endearing cat created by his imagination, who, in the company of an owl, went to sea in a 'pea-green boat'. This cat, like Foss, had dark stripes and, on his tail, six dark rings, but the tail differed from that of Foss by being long and upstanding.

Lear was not alone in instinctively associating owls and cats. In the garden of a Victorian house in West London are two stone figures daubed with lichen and partly hidden by shrubs and rose bushes, representing—or so I thought—owls. But no. One was indeed an owl; the other, it transpired, was a cat. A cat viewed from behind, sitting upright, tail neatly folded, differs little in shape from an owl.

However, the two have more in common than shape. Both are killers of mice, both nocturnal creatures with eyes as mysterious as deep pools, both revered from time immemorial, both attracted by moonlight. It is fitting that Lear's owl should reiterate 'What a beautiful Pussy you are', and that, to celebrate their marriage, the two should dance in the light of the moon.

Charles Baudelaire's love of cats was so strong as sometimes to expose him to ridicule. If a cat crossed the street or appeared in a doorway he would coax her to come to him, take her in his arms, fondle her, sometimes stroke her coat the wrong way. He used to pause at a particular laundry to look at the cat lying curled on a pile of freshly laundered linen. When visiting, he was restless until he had been introduced to the cat. No matter whether he was in a private house or a business establishment, he would pick the cat up, caress her, become so absorbed that, if spoken to, he might have been deaf or a thousand miles away. Some people were affronted at what they considered a breach of good manners; others attributed his behaviour to his being a man of letters and therefore an oddity.

He says of cats, in one of several poems devoted to them in *Les Fleurs du Mal*, that they take up *les nobles attitudes*. Nor has anyone better evoked the quiet strength of cats, their sphinx-like pose, flanks afiire with sparks, eyes starred with gold—their magnetism, their mystery, their affinity with darkness:

> L'Erèbe les eût pris pour ses coursiers funèbres,
> S'ils pouvaient au servage incliner leur fierté.

> Hades would have made them draw his chariot of death
> Could they have bent their pride to be his slaves.

His cat is solace to his anguished spirit:

Viens, mon beau chat, sur mon coeur amoureux;
Retiens les griffes de ta patte,
Et laisse-moi plonger dans tes beaux yeux,
Mêlés de métal et d'agate.

Come, my beautiful cat, lie upon my loving breast;
And keep your claws within their sheaths.
Now let me plunge into your beauteous eyes
Which glint like metal and agate stones.

And again he writes:

Dans ma cervelle se promène
Ainsi qu'en son appartement,
Un beau chat, fort, doux et charmant.
Quand il miaule, on l'entend à peine,

Tant son timbre est tendre et discret;
Mais que sa voix s'apaise ou gronde,
Elle est toujours riche et profonde:
C'est là son charme et son secret.

Within my brain he prowls
As in his private room, a lovely cat
So gentle, strong and full of charm.
One hardly hears him mew,

Because his voice is tenderly discreet;
But let it be serene or vexed,
Still always it is sonorous and profound.
This is his charm and his secret.

Baudelaire remarks, as does St Philip Neri, on the fragrance of a cat's fur. If he caressed a cat but once, he says, he carried the scent upon himself.

But a cat was not merely an attractive creature. He came close to being, in the eyes of Baudelaire, what a *lar* or *genius loci* was to the Romans—a spirit, a divinity presiding over the household:

Peut-être est-il fée, est-il dieu ?

Perhaps he is a spirit, or a god ?

Samuel Butler, when a favourite cat died, could not bear the idea
of getting another ... not for some time. Meanwhile, to be rid of
mice he borrowed a friend's cat, called Prince, 'a love of a cat'.
Prince brought in a stray. The two slept curled up together, looking
'much lovelier' than Prince on his own. A child who was playing
with Prince exclaimed: 'He's got pins in his toes!' The incident
found a place in Butler's *The Way of All Flesh.*

At one time or another **Mark Twain** had at least four cats, with
complicated names which included Blatherskite and Zoroaster—
good practice, he thought, for his children to learn the pronunciation
of difficult words. Cats were constantly in his mind. Looking at the
'velvety backs' of mountains in Honolulu, he wanted to stroke them
as one would stroke 'the sleek back of a cat'. In Colombo he
regretted, in the compound, the absence of a cat .. 'No cat; yet a
cat would have liked this place.' In Bermuda he was pleased to find
no 'plunging, barking dogs', but 'upwards of a million cats!'

Sometimes a cat brings out the more pleasing side of a person's
nature. This was true of **Thomas Hardy.**

The pent-up tenderness in his awkward disposition found an
outlet in his relations with his cat. When the cat died he was overwhelmed with grief: the thought of another animal was unbearable.

Bad enough to recall the familiar voice sounding up the staircase
in the early morning, a paw suspended, or back arched, awaiting a
caress. Better ruthlessly to sweep away traces of the past: tufts of
hair on a chair; pathways scraped among the bushes; the marks of
claws on the trunk of a tree.

But to forget is impossible. From the window where the cat used
to bound on to the sill, the poet saw, under a tree, a small mound
recalling that his friend now lay where once he played.

And yet solace came to Hardy in his last years: a little grey

47

Persian with amber eyes, called Cobby. During the poet's last illness Cobby stayed beside him. After his master's death the little cat disappeared.

In Saha, the feline heroine of *La Chatte*, **Colette** has immortalised the beloved cat which she and her last husband Maurice Goudeket shared: 'the cat we had in common', he says in *Près de Colette*.

They bought her at a cat show—or, as Colette liked to put it, she bought them: a Chartreuse, shapely, four months old, with short, thick fur and yellow eyes, quiet and wise. Spectators, watching Colette's growing interest in this flawless little cat, had urged: 'Buy her, Madame Colette. Buy her!' M Goudeket thought they would need a lead to take her home, but Colette said: 'No, she realises she's mine already.'

They could not find a name for her. They thought of Tahiti,

' "Chatte", she said one day in the garden, "you are forbidden, once for all, to touch those finches." '

because she was the colour of grey pearls; but the cat made it clear that she was to be known solely as La Chatte, or Chatte, 'as though she were the only cat in the world'.

Fond though Colette was of her little black and white French bulldog, she gave precedence to La Chatte. Cats, she felt, though they had once been worshipped, were exposed to hostility to a degree dogs were not and therefore called for a special tenderness and protectiveness. But she did not sentimentalise or resort to non-sensical 'baby' talk. She spoke to La Chatte in French, in deep affection, politely, firmly, making her meaning clear, without raising her voice. 'Chatte,' she said one day in the garden, 'you are forbidden, once for all, to touch those finches.' Chatte lay down on the grass, put in her claws philosophically, and tucked her paws under her. There was no more trouble over the finches.

Colette owed to cats, she said, certain of her own qualities— among them, an aversion to loud, harsh noises; a need for periods of silence; an ability to conceal her feelings. When Chatte died, there was no extravagant show of grief. For a few days Colette was silent, a little withdrawn. But years later her husband would hear her murmuring to herself in a voice of unbearable sadness: 'Oh, that *Cat!*'

Colette's love for cats came to her from Sido, her mother. Not even Sido's heartfelt grief at the death of her husband could quench an impulse of joy when, on the occasion of the burial, a black kitten, tail held high as if he were a full-grown tom, joined the mourners, walking sedately—then suddenly took a leap, scampering, frolicking, falling over himself. 'Oh, look at him!' Sido exclaimed, clapping her hands. 'How funny he is!'

The cats in Colette's writings, non-fiction and fiction, emanate from her own experience. Saha; La Belle Fanchette, who, when her mistress is reading in the library, persists in having two or three volumes of Larousse removed from the shelf to provide a space where she can curl up, her purr, though the glass doors are closed, still audible, 'non-stop, like a muffled drum'; Babou, the 'black devil', as sinuous as an eel, who in the kitchen garden eats asparagus tips and choicest strawberries and inhales deliriously the scent of violets; Kiki-la-Doucette, who in a railway carriage (she hates rail travel) when it is feared she will refuse to return to her basket from which she has been released to enjoy a chicken bone, takes everyone aback: having sat on the seat leisurely washing herself, she stands up, stretches, and with the utmost composure steps back into the basket.

'A cat's merely a cat. But Saha is Saha,' says her owner, the young man Alain, in *La Chatte*.

Yes, Saha is special. She epitomises feline sensitivity. Many is the cat who has pined, grown thin, lost the sheen on his coat, gone off his food, when a new cat has been brought in; he is made to feel hurt, ousted like a child who believes that a younger brother or sister is preferred. But Saha feels she is ousted not by another cat but by Camille, Alain's fiancée and, subsequently, his wife. Already, during the engagement, Saha is out of countenance; she roams the shadowy, moonlit garden uttering a pitiable 'Me-rou-wa . . . Me-rou-wa.' Puzzled, Alain strokes her, feeling a tenderness for her which, he has to confess, he does not feel for Camille. 'She's my cat, my very own cat,' he murmurs. She is his 'beloved cat', his 'little puma'. He goes upstairs to bed, taking Saha with him. When he turns out the light she kneads his chest, a single claw rhythmically piercing the silk of his pyjamas, purring full-throatedly.

After the marriage ceremony Alain leaves Saha in his former home, with his mother. The cat pines, refuses to eat, will not drink her milk; her breathing is shallow, her nostrils burn. Shocked at the change, Alain takes her to the studio flat where he and Camille are living.

Saha adjusts to her surroundings. She sleeps in the bathroom on a cork-covered stool; eats raw liver in the tiny kitchen; sits on a polished ebony table, her blue shape mirrored as in a pool of darkness; balances on a giddy parapet, gazing down, unperturbed, upon the backs of swallows flying below. Her coat has not regained its iridescence, but Saha is 'alive' again.

Yet all is not well. Camille cannot understand, much less accept, Alain's total devotion to Saha: his attentions, his concern, his tender affection. One evening in July when Alain is out, Camille, overwhelmed by resentment, pushes the cat from the parapet. She hears a grating of claws on the rough-cast wall, sees Saha, her body making the shape of an S, clutching the air . . .

Later Alain returns, carrying Saha. She had fallen six floors, landed on the awning of a second floor flat and bounced on to a lawn. There is no sign of bodily injury, but her heart races and from time to time she shivers. Alain asks Camille to feel Saha's head, to see if there are bumps.

At the touch of Camille's hand Saha turns from a gentle, docile cat into a fury: she leaps in the direction of Camille, eyes flaming, teeth bared, fur on end. Alain springs up to keep the two apart. Then he notices, on a piece of paper on which Saha has been standing, spots of moisture: four dots around an irregular central patch. The truth begins to dawn. 'Don't you realise what those footprints mean?' he says to his wife harshly. 'Fear, the sweat of fear. Only fear can cause a cat to sweat.'

That night Alain returns to his mother's home, carrying Saha in a wicker basket. He lets her loose in the garden, goes indoors, comes out again and sits on a step. Reaching out his hand into the darkness he feels Saha's furry body, the touch of her whiskers, her cool nostrils. She smells of musk and geraniums. Trustful, vulnerable, with perhaps ten years to live. Alain's heart aches at the thought of how short is the life of a love so great.

Walter de la Mare evokes both the mystery and the homeliness of cats.

In his short story *Broomsticks*, jet-black Sam is, in the eyes of his mistress, a highly satisfactory cat: intelligent, companionable, punctual, fastidious. Just the cat for a woman living alone in a remote house on the moors.

So it seemed.

Then things began to happen ... Strange, disquieting 'goings on'. Sam was no longer companionable, no longer amenable. At times his face, Miss Chauncey noticed, wore a defiant, secretive expression. The moonlit, lonely moor had bewitched him. Mysterious noises—sounds like the swish of wings or the frou-frou of watered silk—summoned him into the night. Doors and windows closed for no reason; he dashed up the chimney. He was no longer the Sam Miss Chauncey had come to rely upon. His presence was no longer reassuring. It was frightening.

Unlike *Broomsticks*, the poem *Five Eyes*, about three cats in a mill, guarding flour-sacks against rodents, is not sinister. Yet mystery steeps this evocation of Jekkel, Jessop, and one-eyed Jill, as they crouch in the darkness ready to pounce. Squeaks resound from the stacks, the wind moans up the staircase. At daybreak old Hans the miller finds the cats' 'black fur dusted with the pallor of flour'.

Different, again, in the poem *Comfort*, is the tone of quiet companionship shared by man and cat. Each accepts the other, each is accepted by the other. The two sit by the hearth—man wearing his 'sheep's wool coat', cat his 'fur-about', both protected from the night air, the wind howling in the chimney. And again in *Puss*, man and cat share the fireside. Man is reading, his legs outstretched to catch the warmth; puss is lying close to the fire.

In his home on the top of a hill in Havana **Ernest Hemingway** had thirty cats. But more interesting than numbers was his attitude to them. A cat, he said, had 'absolute emotional honesty': human beings, for one reason or another, may hide their feelings, but a cat does not. And since most of us have to admit, if we are sincere, that we like approval, this honesty on the part of the cat can put us at his mercy. We can be 'subject to his judgment' just as we are subject to a monarch.

As to that, Hemingway made the point that unlike dogs, who want to be on maty terms with humans, cats have to be kings and queens. But he was not overawed by their royal status. On the contrary, he felt a special tenderness for them.

He had confidence, too, in the good sense of cats. While living in Paris he and his wife, when they had to be out, left their baby son in the care of a sensible, affectionate, yellow-eyed cat called F. Puss. There was consternation among the neighbours, who thought the cat would surely suffocate the baby. F. Puss, however, sat up erect, like a nanny, keeping guard. On the rare occasions when he slept in the cradle he lay at a distance from the child's head and face.

Writer and Minister of Culture in General de Gaulle's government, **André Malraux** appears as a young man in a photo in which a little tabby sits on his shoulder. Again and again in his writings he turns to cats for his imagery: in Nubia an Egyptian cat, 'as wild and as black as a lynx', follows Queen Sebeth; in India, in the temple of Madurai, a black cat slips into the shadows 'as if he held the secret of the universe'; Nehru moves among the furniture 'like a Siamese cat', gesticulates to the French ambassador's cat 'as if he were stroking her back from a distance'; a diplomat is 'as reticent as a cat'; Chinese children clamber over a tomb 'like cats'; a woman's eyes are 'as blue as the eyes of a Siamese'. And so on.

Malraux was able to draw cats charmingly, in a few bold strokes —rather in the style of Jean Cocteau's cats which decorate the Chapelle de Simples at Milly, near Fontainebleau. Sometimes his signature takes the form of a cat in outline.

At Malraux's funeral a bronze Egyptian cat from the Louvre was displayed.

Eleanor Farjeon's portly, sandy cat was called Benignus after a Franciscan friar of that name. He was very much a creature of routine and, where Eleanor was concerned, inordinately possessive.

Denys Blakelock, the actor, used to spend a weekend from time to time at Eleanor's home in Hampstead, leaving as a rule after tea on Sunday. One weekend, Denys told me, at the last minute, when his suitcase was in the hall and Benignus was sitting solemn as an image, awaiting the moment of departure, he decided to stay until the following morning.

When he picked up his case to go back to his room, Benignus was transformed from his usual placid self into a fiend. Crouching on the lowest step of the stairs, fur on end, he spat at Denys; then, after emitting a single blood-curdling yowl, made a dash for Eleanor's room where he sat in glum silence for the rest of the evening, staring from under the sofa.

In 'The Cat', his poem about a puss who refuses, when called, to come in from the garden, **Richard Church** shows his understanding of feline independence and sheer 'cussedness'.

The cat knows that he can afford to bide his time, for he knows that he is wanted, needed. He hears his mistress calling in the dusk. The moon hangs in the sky, a thin crescent; bats are flittering, and the scent of jasmine is heavy upon the air.

She calls. She calls again. A lonely call. He knows he can 'play it cool'. Shielded by thorny branches, where a gooseberry bush leans over a rose tree, he sits motionless, silently 'gazing down his nose'.

The words call to mind Théophile Steinlen's golden-brown lithograph of a large tabby lying on a wooden balustrade against a backcloth of foliage: relaxed and content, he lies with front paws folded inward, tail and one hind leg hanging down, his half-closed yellow eyes looking down his nose.

Louis MacNeice had a deep affection for cats. Cats, he said, 'leavened the long flat hours' of childhood.

He wrote a moving poem, 'The Death of a Cat'—the more moving because in it he blames himself for the loss and subsequent death in Athens of this 'dancer' and 'joker' with the tail 'like a question-mark at a mast-head':

> this was a person
> In a small way who had touched our lives
> With a whisk of delight, like a snatch of a tune
> From which one whole day derives.

4

Stranger than fiction

The cat at war

During the three and a half years in which Lord Heathfield commanded the siege of Gibraltar against the Spaniards, he inspired with courage not only his troops, but his cats. Despite the roar of the artillery, his beloved cats accompanied him each day when he went the round of the fortifications.

During World War II a little cat (she never grew bigger than a large kitten) attached herself to Richard Austin, the writer, then a young soldier serving in Greece.

She liked, above all else, to be thrown high into the air, land on the top of a cupboard, then let herself drop (no feline rotating of the body), totally relaxed, into hands she knew were waiting to receive her. Then she would purr and rub against the young man's legs, asking for this to be repeated.

At night the little cat slept in one of Richard's military boots, a pair of socks making a cushion.

How many cats have provided the theme for a *Times* leader? On 13 January 1943 Mourka did so: Mourka, the Russian cat who, during the siege of Stalingrad, carried dispatches, concerning gun- emplacements, through the bomb-wrecked streets of the city. Never an error of judgement, never a slip-up.

As always, there were some who sneered. But the writer of the leader took the opportunity to rend those who 'with the cavilling peculiar to vulgar minds' attribute unworthy motives to the great—who, in short, belittled Mourka because it so happened that there was a Company kitchen in the house to which the cat carried the dispatches.

Three cheers for Mourka, who proved himself worthy of Stalin-

'She defied the police, forced her way in and searched until she had retrieved a terrified black tom.'

grad! 'Whether for cat or man,' the article concludes, 'there can be no higher praise.'

During the recent bombing of the headquarters of the National Trust in Ulster, a neighbour went to the aid of the caretakers, who were being hustled out in a state of collapse. She then returned to look for the cat. Despite falling masonry, flames, and warnings from security forces that there might be another unexploded bomb inside, she defied the police, forced her way in and searched until she had retrieved a terrified black tom.

The reaction to her courage comprised, in general, sneers from onlookers for having risked her life to save a 'mere' cat.

In politics

In July 1874, during a debate in the House of Commons on the Public Worship Regulation Bill, Sir William Harcourt, political lieutenant to Mr Gladstone, was startled by a burst of laughter. A large tabby, after coming down the Opposition gangway, leisurely crossed the floor. Then, frightened by the noise, he sprang over the heads of members seated on the ministerial benches below the gangway, and amid shouts of laughter bounded above those on the back benches, until, reaching a side door, he vanished.

At home . . .

Paddy sat on the draining-board purring, while his mistress was washing up. Suddenly a 'thing' zoomed in through the open window. It was long and black, had wings, horns, and legs. It buzzed. Paddy's mistress screamed and dropped a plate.

Paddy rose leisurely to his feet, stretched, yawned, leapt into the air, caught the 'thing' in his mouth and chewed it.

Then he sat down and washed his face.

A housewife coming down one morning to the kitchen heard a rapid tapping sound. On opening the door she saw her cat and, no more than an inch or so away, a starling feeding from the same plate, neither taking notice of the other.

A woman when emptying her washing machine came upon a kitten rolled up in a sheet. Deeply concerned—she feared he was suffocated—she hurried him to the vet, who assured her that the little creature was suffering from no more than a mild attack of dizziness.

Grandpa and pa, sober, solemn, serious-minded men, ardent supporters of Chelsea, were watching on television a match between Chelsea and Manchester United.

The score was even, the atmosphere tense. The two men continued to watch quietly, intently, when in a flash victory went to Chelsea. The excitement of grandpa and pa knew no bounds. With a burst of applause they shouted, laughed, clapped, stamped.

The cat, who had been sitting there minding her own business, affronted by this sudden unseemly din, gave a leap through the open window and landed five floors down, on her four paws, unhurt.

A twelve-year-old cat attempted to raid the nest of a missel-thrush. The parent bird chased her the length of the garden, 'dive-bombing' her, making a terrific din, and even inflicting a wound on the top of her head.

The cat dashed indoors, up the stairs. When, after a week, she ventured into the garden again, the sight of any bird larger than a sparrow sent her rushing back inside. It was some time before she recovered her equanimity.

... and abroad

Wilhelmina the cat, having worked loose the window-catch of a caravan in which she was travelling along the Edgware Road, made her escape.

A taxi driver, seeing what had happened, stopped his cab, ran across the pavement, chased her into a shop, scooped her into his arms and dropped her into the back of his cab. Making a dash through Mayfair he caught up with the caravan, which by then had reached the Hilton Hotel in Park Lane, and handed over the cat to the astonished, delighted owner.

Willy, a marmalade cat in Cincinnati, was addicted to watching bingo, which was played in a nurses' home on Monday evenings from 7.45 until 9.30 pm. Every Monday he set out from home at 7.30, arrived on time and sat on the window-sill, staring through the glass until the end of the session. He was never known to get the day or hour wrong.

In the course of time his name was changed from Willy to Bingo.

A merchant living in Messina noticed his cats, in a state of great excitement, scratching at the door of his room. When he let them out they dashed down the stairs and scratched at the door into the street more violently still. Surprised, their master opened the door and followed them through the streets of the town, out into the country beyond. Even there they were still wild with fright, scratching and tearing the grass.

Presently there was an earthquake shock. Houses, including the one belonging to the merchant, crashed to the ground. Merchant and cats were safe.

Who's who?

Honey Grindle was a ginger tom who liked to sit sunning himself in a Derby bowl on the desk of Geoffrey Handley-Taylor, the first editor of *Who's Who*.

This cat has the distinction of being the first, if not the only, feline to have an 'entry' in the *International Who's Who in Poetry*— a secret shared for almost fifteen years between Handley-Taylor and John Masefield, another lover of cats.

The entry runs:

Grindle (Honey) (Fanny Beckett), born April 21, 1937. Publications: *Roof Poems*, *Cat Fancier's Guide*. Recreations: Bird watching, fishing. Clubs: Manx, Derby Bowl.

Salvaged

During a dustmen's strike in Glasgow the Corporation issued plastic bags which were duly filled with rubbish.

When the strike ended a woman looking out of the window noticed two dustmen in the next-door yard deep in consultation. Presently one went away and returned carrying what appeared to be a piece of old counterpane, took it into the adjoining garden and arranged it into a kind of nest. Then the two of them went away and came back carrying a cluster of newly born kittens which they put into the 'nest', covering them carefully against the cold.

The mother, who up to this point was not to be seen, had chosen for her confinement a sheltered spot among the bags. Presently she appeared. She stood stock still; then, hearing the mewing of her kittens, made straight for them. A moment or two later she reappeared, carrying a kitten by the scruff of its neck. She repeated this procedure until she had transferred all the kittens to a hiding place of her own choosing.

Cats in clover

A cat in Los Angeles who inherited nearly 7,000 dollars in his own right to enable him to continue his gourmet style of living was sent by the Californian officials a tax demand for 608 dollars. He is believed to be the first animal in the United States to receive a tax demand.

The front page of the Austrian paper *Neue Kronen Zeitung* carried, on 29 September 1975, a photograph of Cassius, 'the richest cat in the world'. Sleek, elegant—an immaculate white front and paws—he sits on the lawn in front of the eighteenth-century mansion which he has inherited. Here he is to live and be cared for till the end of his life. This is not, however, in Austria, but in England: in Bath.

A full life . . .

A kitten on a farm at Purton, Gloucestershire, was born blind. At first he blundered about, bumped into doors, collided with furniture.

Then he was 'taken over' by two dogs who accompanied him on walks, saw to it that the way was clear, protected him from intruders, encouraged him, taught him to eat from their own plates. Thanks to their intervention, he grew into a high-spirited cat, confident and sociable, with plenty of initiative.

The prospects for Skippy looked somewhat dim: he was born with three legs.

His mother, however, showing characteristic feline concern for her young, took all the greater care of him, continuing to wash him for five years as though he were still a kitten.

Then, when she died, he began to show initiative and came into his own. He grew into a magnificent animal, measuring a yard from nose to the tip of his tail; he was a splendid fighter when occasion demanded, yet otherwise extremely gentle. As though to compensate for the missing leg, the other three were exceptionally strong.

On the farm

In a part of Ireland where cows were still milked by hand, there was a barn cat, called Patsy, who at milking time used to sit at the side of each cow in turn, her mouth stretched as wide open as possible while she waited for each fresh squirt of milk. Her kittens, who were extremely wild, would not go near the cows. Yet they benefited, from time to time, from the fact that the milkman had a poor aim. Milking over, Patsy, well satisfied, would clamber up to the loft where she sat washing her paws. Meanwhile the kittens licked dry her milk-sodden coat—they, too, well satisfied!

Njel and his wife Gudrun lived on a remote farm in the north-east of Iceland.

Like other Icelandic farmers, Njel had a store or barn where he used to hang lamb and salmon to be smoked before being transferred to the freezer. One day, when Gudrun was busy in the store, she was pestered by their tabby cat who kept circling her legs, getting in her way, pawing the ground, miaowing insistently.

Gudrun went back to the house and gave him some fish. He would not touch it. Annoyed, she picked up the cat, intending to shut him indoors. He struggled free. Then, as she was returning to the store, he tried to bar her way, eyes glinting, back arched, tail lashing. Exasperated, Gudrun pushed past him and went in.

At that moment, as she reached up for a leg of lamb, the cat made a lunge in her direction, emitting a blood-chilling yowl. It was too late. A mink had slipped out from under a pile of logs and attacked Gudrun. Her screams brought the dogs, but they were too frightened to put up a fight. The cat, on the other hand, went for the mink again and again, but was powerless to drive it off.

Farm-hands came to Gudrun's rescue, and she was rushed by helicopter to hospital where she was treated for severe blood poisoning, shock and depression. But for the cat's intervention she would have been dead: her legs were scarred for life.

This is the story as told by Njel and Gudrun.

A Gloucester family

The mother, a long-haired black and white cat, belonged to a pork butcher in Gloucester; the father, a ginger tom, to the greengrocer next door. Each time a litter of kittens was due the tom systematically collected orange papers out of a dustbin and constructed a kind of nest in a wooden box. At a later stage the parents carried the kittens, one at a time, to the seclusion of a cellar below a grocer's shop across the road.

One of the kittens, a ginger like his father, had a passion for sculling on the canal. Unable to resist the temptation to walk along the scull, he sometimes toppled into the water. This did not trouble him, however: he simply swam ashore. As a reward, he used to be given a saucer of warm milk. He preferred to drink this sitting up at the table with the family, his forepaws resting on the cloth.

'The mother, a long-haired black and white cat, belonged to a pork butcher in Gloucester; the father, a ginger tom, to the greengrocer next door.'

The Agha's companion

Females, human and otherwise, are debarred from Mount Athos, which history and tradition have allotted to monasteries of the Orthodox Church.

Over a century ago Robert Curzon, later Lord Zouche, when he broke his journey at the quarters of the Agha, or Turkish commander, resident on the peninsula, noticed that the Agha's sole companion was a cat. Nothing strange in that. But next morning, at breakfast, the cat appeared accompanied by two kittens.

'What!' Curzon exclaimed, 'A *she*-cat on Mount Athos? And kittens, too!'

'Hush!' said the Agha. 'A she-cat indeed. I brought her from Stamboul. She reminds me of my home, my wife, and my children. But not a word! Or they'll take her from me.'

Curzon felt sad as he rode away, glancing back from time to time at the Agha, his cat sitting at his side. He would have liked to take Agha, cat, all of them, away with him—so lonesome and melancholy the poor man looked!

5
Cats of character

Perseus

Name: PERSEUS Quantocks. Age: 9. Colour: Seal point. Breed: Siamese. Favourite occupation: Observing *homo sapiens*. Abominations: Enoch the black cat from the village. Address: c/o BBC, London.

This is Perseus, the cat familiar to the many listeners who hear John Ebdon's talks on Radio Four.

'Is your cat Perseus *real*?' The question was put to John by an elderly lady at the Cheltenham Festival of Literature, after he had been talking for an hour or so. She had not been listening, she explained, for one thing alone occupied her mind: 'Is Perseus, the cat mentioned on the radio, *real*?'

Then at Christmas, when Perseus, despite the increase in postal charges, received a stack of cards and John three, one of the latter raised the question, somewhat belligerently: 'Why, if Perseus is real, do we not hear him, and not only *about* him?'

Yes, the question recurs—the implication being, presumably, that Perseus is a mere product of John Ebdon's imagination. To some extent he is. Are we not, all of us, moulded by the opinions, ideas, imagination, of friends, acquaintances, relations? But that does not detract from our reality: it simply colours, to some degree, the nature of this reality.

To clear the air, John Ebdon has explained that he and Perseus, in private, use the English language to communicate with each other, even on abstruse matters. *In private*. For although John has an open mind on the subject, Perseus is absolutely adamant that their conversations be strictly between themselves.

To forestall any who, dissatisfied with this explanation, might continue to cast suspicion on the reality of Perseus, John has taken two steps. First, he permits his cat's raucous, strident, characteristically Siamese voice to be heard on a cassette. Secondly, he has allowed a photograph of Perseus, along with his sister Capella and John himself, to appear in the *Radio Times*. For this much publicity he has, he assures us, the permission of Perseus who, like Oscar Wilde, is of the opinion that there is only one thing worse than being talked about, and that is *not* being talked about!

Perseus is a handsome cat, his cream coat set off with chocolate brown. His mask is brown; so is his long aristocratic nose; so are his shell-like ears, his slender, gloved paws. His blue eyes are clear, bright, alert.

First and foremost, Perseus is a 'character', with a phenomenal intelligence, strong likes and dislikes, and a mind of his own.

He abhors Enoch, the black cat in the village. Scarcely less abhorrent to him is a human with whom he is familiar, by the name of Clive, who displays, vocally, some of the less attractive feline traits. Remarkably observant of human beings, Perseus finds them, alternately, amusing and terrifying. A recurrent nightmare of his is that he has evolved into a *Homo sapiens*. Cocktail parties he finds a bore: so many people talking yet saying nothing. It was during one of these that he sidled up to John (he was squinting, which showed that he was livid), sat down and, putting his left rear leg behind his ear—it looked like an abandoned aircraft gun—pointed to one of the guests from whose clutches he had just escaped. This woman, sweeping him off his feet and holding him within six inches of her face, had gushed: 'Boo . . . ful, boo . . . ful, boo . . . ful boy!' . . . and so forth.

The rapport between man and cat is obvious both in the photograph and in the way in which John Ebdon speaks about Perseus. One thing only I find hard to accept. 'He can do without me,' John says, 'but I could not do without him.' Without John—without his interest, his encouragement, his affectionate, intimate tone of voice, Perseus would not be the same cat. Cats, despite a reputation for independence, are more in need of friendship and affection than is sometimes apparent.

The Churchill cats

'I purred like a cat,' Sir Winston Churchill said, so pleased was he by the welcome given to him during his journey in 1954 from Washington to Ottawa. He could not have said more, for he loved cats.

65

Whenever he called at 10 Downing Street during the Munich crisis he would be seen, before he went in, bending down to stroke his friend Bob, the black and white cat who, in the words of Christabel Lady Aberconway, 'held the steps of No 10'. Again, whenever he went aboard a ship he immediately asked to be introduced to the cat.

A marmalade tom of his is immortalised in six drawings, showing the cat in a variety of poses, made in 1933 by the late Sir William Nicholson and given by him to Lady Churchill.

Sir Winston particularly liked marmalade cats. In a photograph taken at the wedding of his grandson in 1964 he appears with one such animal, called Jock. There is a cut-out picture of Jock at Blenheim Palace, in the room in which Sir Winston was born, and at Chartwell pictures of him are sold in aid of the RSPCA.

Another cat to whom Sir Winston was devoted was a black one, Nelson, who lived originally at Admiralty House and was then taken to Downing Street when Sir Winston became Prime Minister. Nelson used to make his appearance in the Cabinet Room, where—so I have been assured—a chair was kept for him next to the Prime Minister. A place was certainly reserved for him at the dining-room table. Sir Eric McClaggan, invited one day to lunch, was delighted to find that the seat beside his was being kept for Nelson!

Sir Winston used to comment on political matters to his cats, addressing whichever of them was present as 'Cat' or 'Mr Cat' or 'My dear'.

He often had a cat on his bed when he was working in the morning. One day in 1943, while convalescing from influenza, he was visited by a Minister. Nelson was lying at the foot of the bed. 'That cat', said Churchill, 'is doing more for the war effort than you are! He acts as a hot-water bottle and saves fuel and power!'

Black humour

Sir William Nicholson, himself a cat lover, was 'taken over' while living at La Rochelle by Black, a 'clown of a cat', tall and round-eyed, who walked in one day uninvited.

This cat not only joined in any game that was being played, but introduced games of his own. A favourite came to be known as 'The Chase'. Nicholson's apartment comprised four rooms—kitchen, salon, dressing-room and bedroom—then a passage leading back to the kitchen. Black's game was to chase or be chased from room to room until the circuit was complete, then begin again—preferably first thing in the morning! If you did not co-operate he would jump on to the bed, bounce up and down, and yowl with frustration until he got his way.

Less strenuous but scarcely less intriguing was the 'spinning' game invented by Nicholson, who had a bowl some two feet across made of elmwood. Black used to clamber into the bowl, then lie stretched out while Nicholson made it spin. Round and round it went, Black lying on his side in ecstasy.

The maid idolised Black, calling him *mon fils*. Sometimes in error she called him Mimi, which infuriated him. At the sound of the word he streaked out of the room. Once, he was missing all day. Eventually he was unearthed from beneath an eiderdown where he had been sleeping.

Yellow eyes

'Scoobie is a large, grey, muscular tabby, partly Siamese, with lots of thick fur and very fine, long whiskers. He is temperamental and a bit aggressive, hates being picked up unless he is in a good mood. Except for an occasional visit next door, he goes no further than the garden. He eats coley.

Scoobie has yellow eyes.

Sandy is very heavy, soft to touch, and has a quantity of thick, rich, ginger-coloured fur. He rarely leaves the garden. Sandy loves Mum and likes to be picked up. He eats meat as well as coley. The first time he saw a mouse he ran away!

Sandy has yellow eyes.

Twiggy is a small brown tabby with a soft, silky coat. She eats coley and meat, and plays with mice. She is a bit moody. Twiggy is very much Annabel's cat.

Twiggy has yellow eyes.

Samson and Delilah are twin kittens. Samson is black, Delilah tortoiseshell. Samson is quite large and formidable, Delilah small and lovable. Both enjoy catching things and will eat anything! Samson is wild, ramps round the garden, never learning anything. Delilah ramps round house and garden, but is gentle, likes company, licks your face and hands and wags her tail like a dog. She gets in a terrible fuss if she loses Samson!

Samson and Delilah have yellow eyes.'

Annabel Redhead, aged 13

A publisher's cat

'Having managed others in the office during the day I go home at night to be managed by my cat. I know that if she jumps on my lap or licks my nose in affection or comes for a short walk, it will be because she wants to—that if it is too cold to walk to a neighbouring house her insistence on going by car will be hard to resist.

My family were all against my having a Siamese. "Siamese are fierce," they chorused. "Siamese do untold damage." "Siamese have horrible voices." But I had seen the advertisement in the local paper, and that was that.

'One pigeon's egg—brought in Sara's mouth and batted around the kitchen floor—heralded the arrival of a nestful of newly born pigeons.'

I soon discovered about the voice. On the way home from the breeder, Sara, eight inches in length, was silent only as long as I was holding her paw. The moment I took my hand out of the basket to change gear a fearful cacophony echoed around the car.

We discovered other things too. They included her readiness to hiss at the largest of dogs, and, if I accidentally frightened her, to "take me on"—jumping into the air from my lap, hissing into my face, fur on end, tail as wide as her slender body.

The household was organised around Sara. This did not only mean persistently opening and closing doors to enable her to be on the right side. It involved removing all kinds of creatures, living and dead! Baby rabbits under the bed; a squirrel in the sink; a stoat in the children's brick box—the news of which sent two burly Devon farmers down the drive for fear they would be asked to help remove it. Not to mention endless mice and, regrettably, birds.

The arrival of one baby rabbit meant we were in for a litter within the next few days. One pigeon's egg—brought in Sara's mouth and batted around the kitchen floor—heralded the arrival of a nestful of newly born pigeons.

She did not catch dogs; she merely tormented them. She would run up a post, wait until a large black dog passed underneath, then jump on its back and swing from its tail. She did the same to a stray sheep we were trying to drive out of the grounds.

There is also Sara's life in the family: her companionship; her habit of lying upside down on my lap; her alertness in learning to type; her confusion when, having been scolded for trying, while the piano was being played, to climb the chimney above a fire burning in the grate, she assumed, ever after, that the sound of the piano was a signal to do just this!

Above all, she takes it for granted that what is ours is hers and what is hers is ours. She is as likely to come and make friends if hit by the newspaper as she is if cajoled. Telephone calls are as much for her as for the rest of us—as many a caller has been astonished to learn. In youth she wandered far and wide, making friends with people as they walked across the fields.

Talk of the ferocity of Siamese cats goes on . . . We have heard mothers warning their offspring against fraternisation. Sara used to jump into neighbours' cars and as a result had all kinds of adventures. In maturity she prefers the back ledge of one particular car, where she crouches, making faces at drivers who are following. At home she is increasingly content just to watch. Yet even in old age she occasionally dashes from under the stairs to trip one of us up—and, when she succeeds, actually laughs aloud!

We have shared a lot. And it has been a richer relationship than would have been possible with a dog, whose anxiety to please would have been greater. With Sara, each day brings something new: pleasure; pride; a desire to be together—this combined with female cussedness; broken crockery; being wakened, if we want to sleep late on a Sunday morning, by her patrolling up and down the terrace; her pretending, too, when we are looking for her, that she is not there—not to mention her howling at 3 am when shut in a spare bedroom!'

Mr David St John Thomas

Fred of Chelsea

'My wife Julia and I have a friend living with us: a big tom. Or do we live with him? Certainly he is undisputed monarch. We address him as Fish-face, Fiend, Softy, Tetra-pod ... etc ... etc. And simply as Fred—which is his name.

Whatever our mode of address the response is the same: total indifference. His coat is snowy white, splotched with black; his weight, around 16 lb, which is hardly surprising, for he has a meal about every twenty minutes. Hence the appellation "cow-shaped", bestowed upon him by an American; for there is no denying that Fred's receding form, with its convex sides, resembles that of a cow.

You have to understand the psychology of Fred. Before taking up residence with us he had been a stray: thin, grubby, his coat a murky grey—perhaps he had slept in coal-sheds? But he must have been good at begging, for he did not look seriously undernourished. Nevertheless those days left a scar (that is why I mention psychology) which can only be healed by the presence on the kitchen floor of at least three dishes of food—not to mention another three in the kitchen belonging to Julia's mother, which is directly below ours.

When Fred first came we had an elegant female called Wig, a silver-grey tabby with a spotless white front and clear green eyes. She was not averse to Fred's attentions, provided these were out of doors, and in due course kittens were born—bright-faced kittens, whose white coats, splotched with black, left no doubt as to who was their father.

Wig, however, would not allow Fred indoors for more than an hour or so at a time. The best he could do was to take his chance, when we were out, make a dash through the cat-flap, clear up Wig's dishes—and away!

When Wig was killed in the traffic, we did our best to dismiss a horrible suspicion that Fred had deliberately pushed her under a car; for the fact is that on the day of her death he took possession of the house, unmoved, it appeared, by her absence . . .

Of late, we have seen him back away when confronted by a mouse. And in the mews he sits unperturbed by the pigeons and they by him. Is his hunting instinct declining as age takes its toll? Or is Isaiah's vision becoming a reality: "They shall not hurt nor destroy in all my holy mountain, said the Lord"?'

Mr Dudley Jones

The Great Mr Thomas

'Old pussy Steer', as Wilson Steer, the painter, used to be called, acquired, when living in Chelsea, a black and white cat known as Mr Thomas. This cat died in 1906 and was succeeded by a fine tabby brought up from the country, a gentle cat with 'paws as soft as clouds', who was given the name Mr Thomas II or The Great Mr Thomas.

The Great Mr Thomas could do no wrong: even when he broke a Sèvres vase he was forgiven. A chair was reserved for him at the dining-room table. If a guest inadvertently sat on it the cat would jump noiselessly on to the table and sit staring at the offender until the embarrassed Steer was driven to saying: 'I'm sorry, I'm afraid you are sitting in Mr Thomas's chair.'

During a holiday in the country Steer befriended a famished half-grown farm cat. He coaxed her to take Bovril, walked two miles to buy liver for her, and at the end of his stay took her back to Chelsea, by that time a plump, contented puss.

Steer's last cat was another tabby who enjoyed himself chasing seagulls on the mudflats in front of the house.

Calculating cat

'Rufus Puss, nearly twenty-one years old, is black, with a short under-coat that is tawny red in places. When he was young the red was specially noticeable on top of his head. Imagine a dark-skinned human with red hair!

He is an extremely intelligent, indeed a calculating, cat, disposed, also, when occasion offers, to take advantage of darkness.

My wife and I wondered why the bath was scratched. Then, disturbed one night, we saw what Rufus was up to: we watched him jump on to the rim at the curved end of the bath, then slither down the sloping enamelled surface!

His detestation of my mother-in-law, to whom he made himself a persistent nuisance, reached its zenith when during the first night of a visit from her he plastered the floor outside her room—("He looks as if he were measuring something," my wife had said earlier in the evening)—with pieces of fish-skin, at a distance of about four inches one from another, so that our visitor could not fail to tread on them when she attempted to go along the passage during the night. Next morning she went home.

When Rufus wants to sit on the chair which I am occupying, he yowls to be let out the door; then, the moment I stand up, nips into my place!

If he cannot get in from the garden through a window, he thumps on the front door.

On two occasions, when a burglar was attempting to break in, he has wakened us in the night. When, therefore, my brother and his wife stayed in our house while we were abroad, we told them to pay heed if at any time Rufus tried to attract their attention. However, they ignored his yowls in the night, and found, in the morning, that their car which had been parked outside the house had been stolen.

When Rufus was three an owlet came and lived with us for some weeks, following us from place to place. Rufus was in attendance, but when the bird sat back on its stumpy tail and extended its claws, he had the sense to avoid an encounter.

He is great friends with Cinder the dog, aged sixteen. The two "gang up" against humans, and keep at bay feline and canine intruders. One day there was a terrific fight between Rufus and two terriers. The terriers fled, bleeding. Then I saw Rufus Puss lying on a flower-bed, as stiff as a poker. I thought all was finished. The stiffness, however, was due not to rigor mortis but to sheer fury!'

Mr A. S. Brettell

Sibil

She began life as a stray, a tiny unwanted kitten who, as can happen, developed greater initiative and ingenuity than many a pampered aristocrat. Given to Mr Sydney Farmer of Oakley Gardens, Chelsea, and named after Dame Sybil Thorndike, she lavished affection upon her owner and was loved no less in return.

Partly Abyssinian, but with the stripes and rings on her thick grey coat that are associated with the best tabbies, she grew into a large handsome cat, her whiskers long and bushy, her eyes intelligent and clear. So amusing were her ways that adults and children called to watch her 'goings-on'.

Her most spectacular performance was the skeleton game. Mr Farmer had a little skeleton made of rubber, and when he pressed a miniature ball at the end of a tube the arms and legs danced up and down. Sibil had watched the skeleton being put away into a drawer in the bureau. She did not forget. Some weeks later Mr Farmer said to her: 'I'll send the skeleton after you!' In a flash Sibil was on the desk, persevering until she had opened the drawer, scooped out the skeleton, played with it and flung it on the floor. This became a regular pastime.

One day a visitor, in the course of conversation, used the phrase 'a skeleton in the cupboard'. Sibil, apparently asleep on a chair the far side of the room, stood up, stretched, sprang on to the bureau and got out her toy in the usual way.

Independent as any cat, she nevertheless carried out implicitly certain orders of her master. 'Get into your box, Sibil.' In she would go. 'That's not your chair, Sibil.' Down she would spring. When he brought her plate of food he would say: 'One, two, three!' At these words she would jump three times into the air. Then, and only then, did she settle down to her meal.

Another command was: 'Cycle up hill, Sibil!' Thereupon Sibil would lie on the floor, flat on her side, pedalling with her legs. At the word 'Faster!' her movements would speed up. If she heard her master say: 'What has the Labour government done to *The Times*?'

she would pounce on the newspaper and tear it with her claws.

Sibil's sense of time enabled her to be awaiting punctually on Sundays the return of her master from the Church of the Holy Redeemer. A minute or two before he was visible or audible Sibil would spring on to the window-ledge, hold the curtain aside with her paw and stare out.

She had, it was agreed, a devotion to St Thomas More. At the sound of his name she would jump on to the mantelpiece, her back to the room, and stare engrossed at a small relic of More's hair-shirt resting against the wall.

Sibil is the only cat I have known who took pleasure in wearing hats. The signal was: 'Sibil, do you want to get ready for Ascot?' whereupon she would jump on to the table and sit purring while her elegant hat was adjusted. A favourite was a rose-pink, low-crowned hat which rested neatly between her ears, the gay colour accentuating the limpid green of her eyes.

Sibil lived to be over twenty. She is remembered as a much loved member of the family.

Jacques le Tricheur

'James Dodger, or Jacques le Tricheur as my wife and I sometimes call him, is a handsome black cat with a white "undercarriage". He is very much a "person", so much has he to say for himself and so well does he understand what is said to him. Demonstrative, he immediately, on coming into the room, puts his paws around our necks, kisses us or bites our chins.

Like many cats, he drinks water from a running tap; but before doing so he "tests" the drips with his paw, in case he has chosen the hot tap instead of the cold. The only other water he'll drink is kept in a mug at the side of our bed: it is known as "Wizard's Water", since, for James, it seems to have some magic property. Also, last thing at night he demands a saucer of warm milk. At the words "Magic Milk" he dashes upstairs and waits for it to be brought to him: he won't touch it downstairs!'

Lord Barclay de Tolly

The Christmas card cat

Each year at the beginning of December, the headmistress of a little church school in Great Yarmouth explained, the children in the art class were asked to design a Christmas card for 'someone special'. She and the staff had been bewildered by an avalanche of cards addressed not to 'Mum' or one of the family or a pop star, but to Gilbert. As a cat's face appeared again and again, they concluded that Gilbert must be a cat. And a very special cat he turned out to be.

Rejected at birth by his mother, he had found attention, comfort, and affection among not his own kind but humans. Made welcome as a kitten by Mrs Marjorie Hunt and her husband, and fed by means of a fountain-pen filler, he gradually grew into a large black cat with a luxurious coat, a white ruff, and a waving tail. Basking in the sunshine and in the attention of passers-by, he would sit on the wall outside the cottage, holding court with delighted children who would talk to him, stroke him, or give him a lick from an ice-cream cornet.

Little boys were his special love. When a group were playing in the street he was likely to be among them. On Saturdays they would call for him and he would race alongside them to the recreation ground where they played football. When tired, he would be brought home on the shoulders of one of the boys. He was their mascot.

On his birthday the family was inundated with sticky-handed callers bringing scraps of chicken, sweets and sugar mice. On the rare occasions when he was unwell, neighbours brought Brand's Essence and slices of chicken breast.

As to dogs, Gilbert would have no nonsense. An Alsatian whimpered in fear when Gilbert seized a bone from him, and, when the dog made half-hearted attempts to get it back, growled menacingly, clinging to the bone, egged on by boys yelling: 'Good old Gilbert! Don't give it to him, Gilbert!'

Then Gilbert took to walking into classrooms. This distracted the children, so it was asked that he should be kept at home during school hours. His timing was flawless. Every afternoon, at ten minutes to four, he would go to meet the children. If by some chance he was shut in at home, he would scrabble frantically at the door or windows to be let out. Neighbours would set their watches by Gilbert when they saw him racing up to the school. As the children came out, he greeted them with mews and purrs of pleasure.

Finally the headmistress conceded that when the weather was bad he might come into the classroom. After a while he did this regularly. His behaviour was impeccable. He would sit quietly, his green eyes looking up at the teacher, happy in the company of his human friends.

Passepartout

'Passepartout sits on my mother's shoulder. Only on my mother's shoulder—nobody else's. And only on her left shoulder.

Passepartout is a peculiar cat.

He won't drink water from a saucer—only in the bathroom, from the bath, the bidet or the basin.

Passepartout is a peculiar cat.

Whatever the temperature, he spends much of the day in the airing cupboard, lying on my father's freshly ironed shirts.

Passepartout is a peculiar cat.

On a summer day, if he spots flies or wasps, he begins to miaow in a strange, stammering note, leaps into the air chasing them. Some he catches and eats, others he leaves half-chewed around the house.

Passepartout is a peculiar cat.

In a crazy mood he dashes all over the house, running so fast that he sways from side to side, finally seeking refuge in the bath. One day he leapt into it, not realising that it was full of water, then scrambled out dripping all over.

Passepartout is a peculiar cat.

If you are alone in the house he springs on to your lap to keep you company, purrs and kneads his claws.

Passepartout is a peculiar cat.'

Jackie Gazzi, aged 13

Carlito the traffic warden

'In Spain, I acquired Carlito: a little tabby and white cat with brilliant blue eyes and a vociferous cry that betrayed Siamese origins.

Coming out of the sea after an early swim I saw a peasant woman trying to submerge a struggling bundle. From her curses, punctuated by piercing miaows, I realised that the bundle was a cat which, presumably, she was intending to drown.

Seething with indignation I grabbed hold of her and released the cat, who dashed off. In fact, it transpired, the woman's intention was not to drown the cat, but to rid him of fleas. In any case, she seemed glad to see the last of him, and went her way along the shore, shrugging her shoulders and muttering.

Presently, having searched in vain, I was astonished to see the cat cowering in the doorway of our home across the road from the beach. Our little maid Carmen, who loved animals, besought me to keep him. Already an injured dog had been installed who, the vet said, was unlikely to survive. A cat might make things worse.

I was thinking along these lines when Carmen called out excitedly that Bonny (the dog) had found a nurse. The cat had walked straight up to the invalid and, wrinkling his pink nose, rubbed it affectionately against the nose of the dog; then, purring loudly, had thrust his head against the dog's side. From that day the invalid began to recover.

The two were inseparable, even sharing at night the same basket. Soon the dog was well enough to walk along the shore, the cat accompanying him, swearing and spitting if another dog approached. So they kept each other company, the one protecting the other.

Our home was at a corner on a busy main road running between the promenade and the beach. Carlito was an unusual cat in that he enjoyed the beach. He used to roll in the sand and bring back tokens of appreciation which were not, I fear, always welcome: putrid sardines, dead crabs, fish heads and so on. And there was always the dread that in crossing the road Carlito would be killed. Carmen laughed at my fears and, as it turned out, she was justified.

One day from the balcony I witnessed a remarkable sight. A policeman in dazzling white uniform halted a convoy of traffic, while a crowd gathered to watch, then beckoned majestically. Who, I wondered, was the august person about to cross? Was it El Caudillo visiting the neighbourhood? Surely no head of government in Europe made so many lightning swoops as did El Generalissimo and his wife!

Imagine, then, my astonishment at seeing the small figure of

Carlito stalking across the road, the tip of his tail waving slightly in appreciation. The policeman bowed, the crowd cheered, the traffic proceeded to roar ahead. Two hours later Carlito ran nimbly up the slope from the beach, squeezed under the railings and waited. Again the policeman halted the traffic, allowing Carlito and a group of children to cross.

The next day there was a ring at the door. The policeman was ushered in. Smiling disarmingly, he begged me not to spoil my "perfect English complexion" by getting sunburnt; said how delighted people were to have foreigners living among them—they called us *nuestros extranjeros*; asked how we liked Spanish fare. The wine? *Licores?* Fish? And so on.

Finally he came to the point. He had been approached by the local school to borrow Carlito to teach the children "kerb-drill". The road, he explained, was a perpetual danger to children crossing to and from the beach. All *niños* were impatient—God could not be looking at everyone at once—he has only one pair of eyes. But this little cat was so *clever*, so *careful*: he set a wonderful example, etc, etc.

The next day Carlito was thrust protestingly into a basket and, accompanied by police, local dignitaries, a couple of priests and a bevy of nuns, conveyed to the school. His performance was admirable. I can still hear the children shouting: "No, not yet!" "Come back!" "Wait till Carlito crosses!" Not once did he let them down.'

Mrs Marjorie Hunt

Khalid and Khan

'In our cottage we have an inglenook fireplace where in winter we burn logs.

One evening I was watching television when Khalid, our Red Burmese, who had been asleep on a chair, suddenly stood up, came over and, putting his forepaws on the settee on which I was sitting, began to sniff. So persistent was he that I got up and, looking around, saw smoke rising from between the cushions. A smouldering ember had shot out of the fire on to the settee without my noticing.

Another day I was painting the bathroom when in came Khalid, in a state of distress, crying persistently. Remembering there was a large fire burning in the lounge I went downstairs and found a log, which had fallen out of the grate, smouldering on the mat.

Twice Khalid had averted what could have been a disastrous fire. Khan, the Blue Burmese, liked boiled rabbit for breakfast.

One morning when he was eighteen months old my daughter Lucretia, who was to have fed him, overslept. She was wakened by a bumping noise which to her consternation (she was alone in the cottage) seemed to come nearer and nearer. Suddenly the curtain across the alcove in which she was sleeping was pushed aside and there stood Khan, gripping in his mouth the lid of a saucepan. His patience at an end, he had jumped on to the cooker, taken the lid off the saucepan in which the rabbit was simmering and carried it by the handle up the stairs—no easy task, since the lid was heavy and the staircase narrow and winding.

When he was three years old, Khan was hit by a passing car and a hind leg was broken. The leg was in plaster for ten weeks. By the end of three, not only could Khan walk—he used to knock on the door with the plastered leg, indicating that he wanted to be let in.'

Mrs S. T. C. Luke

The cat in the White House

According to Jacob Riis's book *Slippers: the White House Cat*, President Theodore Roosevelt's pet used to disappear for days and weeks at a time, yet never failed to be back at the White House for a diplomatic or other important dinner.

One night when the glittering procession was moving out of the State Dining Room, led by the President supporting on his arm the wife of a distinguished ambassador, Slippers lay stretched full length in the middle of the corridor. The President, hesitating for a moment while he gave a sidelong glance at his companion, stepped aside to avoid inconveniencing Slippers. The others had no choice but to follow the President's example.

Persians sans pareil

'I was nine years old when I was given a white Persian with china-blue eyes and a thick fluffy coat, who slept at the foot of my bed, under the coverlet. Then one morning I woke to find no longer one cat, but a cat and four kittens! Her long, luxurious fur had concealed the fact that she was on the verge of motherhood.

That was many years ago. Now my husband and I have two Persians: Yasmin, who is blue, and Bubsy, who is smoke-coloured— a delicate silvery shade, like the inside of an oyster-shell. Both came to us as kittens. First, Yasmin; a month later, Bubsy. Yasmin ruled the house. She strutted about, her amber eyes shining with mischief, tail swaying as she walked. Or she would wriggle on her back along my arm, toes extended to be tickled.

Wardrobe doors had to be left open so that she could sleep inside a shoe. Day began at four am. I would feel her weight upon my chest, hear her purr, throbbing like a drill. A paw would play with my hair, a whisker brush my face.

One day Yasmin was missing. We searched, under furniture, in cupboards . . . in vain. Then we caught sight of her curled inside a painted china bowl, too small to be seen above its rim. Today, fully grown, she still sleeps in this bowl. If it has been moved, she won't rest until she has found it.

She spent a night with us in a hotel in Harrogate. Awake at day-break, she gave the night porter no peace until he produced a saucer of warm milk.

Yasmin had been with us a month when I bought Bubsy. I saw him at a cat show, standing on his hind legs, beating hell out of a ball hanging on a string. Yasmin was not pleased to see this intruder, but Bubsy had a generous, gentle nature, and within a fortnight Yasmin was madly in love with him. It was a joy to watch them playing together with ping-pong balls and pieces of string. One morning we woke to see Bubsy climbing the curtains, Yasmin following.

The two are up to all sorts of tricks. Yasmin, when she hears the key in the door, rolls on her back, paws the air. She does the same, only more quickly, when she wants to be fed.

Putting clean sheets on a bed is for the cats an invitation to play "bed-mice". As soon as the bottom sheet is on, they jump up and, when the top sheet comes down over them, are enthralled—all those wrinkles to chase!

As to the bathroom, Yasmin, when she hears the water running, picks her way along the edge of the bath, deliberating whether to sit by the taps or lie on a box of tissues in a rack from which she can dip a paw into the water. She does not mind getting wet; she leaves the bathroom with coat and tail dripping. But there can be no question of having a bath until Bubsy has been removed from the place where he likes best of all to sleep—in the empty bath!

When we take the cats to the office, that is quite a "thing"! Whereas Yasmin, like Colette's Kiki-la-Doucette, steps demurely into her basket, Bubsy dashes under the bed—this is his "game"—from where I have to extricate him while my husband holds up the bedstead!

At the office the two have a splendid time. Everyone makes a fuss of them. And there are stationery cupboards and filing baskets in which to sleep. Or a coat flung across a chair—especially if it is fur or suede—provides an ideal "cushion". There are pens to grab; and to watch the golfball typewriter functioning is entrancing!

They are a wonderful pair of cats and lead a most exciting life.'
Mrs Koraly Hamilton Northen

Tabby Puss, Black Puss and Furry Puss

Biddy Darlow, an artist friend of mine, was sitting in the firelight with her little son Jeremy. Outside the wind howled. Rain came bucketing down, lashing the window-panes. Through the roar of the wind and the lash of the rain, Biddy heard a faint miaow. She went to the door, opened it, and saw a cat—one of the cats from the nearby farm—carrying a kitten in her mouth. The cat put down the kitten, laying it in a puddle immediately outside the door, then turned and went.

'What a way to treat her kitten!' Biddy said to herself, picked up the little creature, dried it and put it into a cardboard box lined with newspaper, close to the fire.

She had scarcely done so when she heard another miaow. Again the cat was at the door, carrying a kitten. Again she put it down in the puddle and went away. Biddy put the kitten in the box with the first one.

Minutes passed and there was a third miaow. This time the cat did not put the kitten down. She walked in, carrying it. Presently there were four cats in the box by the fire: the mother and three kittens.

Mother puss had found a home in which to bring up her family.

The kittens were distinct in appearance and personality. One was tabby, one black, and one tortoiseshell. The first two had short fur, the third a rather long coat. They came to be known as Tabby Puss, Black Puss and Furry Puss.

Tabby Puss was handsome and a bit of a 'boss'. Disinclined to do anything for himself, he sat letting the others wash his coat.

Black Puss was small, and not at all handsome—in fact he was rather ugly; but he was by far the most intelligent.

Furry Puss, with her fluffy coat and distinctive markings, was the prettiest of the three, and had an affectionate nature.

Homes were found for Tabby Puss and Black Puss, but Furry Puss, Jeremy's favourite, remained.

Sadie and company

As soon as Mrs Cadogan opened the wicker basket, out leapt the kitten, giving what almost seemed a whoop of joy, made straight for a patch of sunlight on the carpet and lay down, rolling ecstatically.

The relationship between Mrs Cadogan and Sadie, as the kitten came to be called, had begun some weeks previously. Walking along a quiet street in a Sussex country town, Mrs Cadogan was passing a Pets' Rescue Centre, its cages out on the pavement, when suddenly she was jerked to a halt. For a moment she thought her dress had caught on a wire projecting from one of the cages. Turning round she saw that her sleeve was indeed caught—not, however, by wire, but by the claws of a kitten's paw thrust between the bars of the cage. No sooner had she managed to free herself than out came a second paw and again she was 'hooked'!

The kitten, her blue eyes opening and closing, purred noisily. If a home was not found within a week or so she would be handed over to the RSPCA, to be put to sleep . . . And so the little orange and white Manx 'stumpie', her tail no bigger than a rabbit's scut, her bright eyes changing from blue to gold, won Mrs Cadogan's heart.

The energy of Sadie was boundless. She 'nagged' her new-found owner into playing games up and down the staircase. Up and down. Up and down. She would bring in her mouth a small rubber ball, drop it at her mistress's feet to be thrown for her, then bring it back, time and again. Mrs Cadogan, to get some peace, had to shut the kitten in. But that did not work: the little creature would bawl incessantly.

Next, Sadie attached herself to the cats next door: Jonathan, a magnificent orange tom, and Fred his brother, a ginger tabby, both mature adults. She adored Jonathan: trailed after him, wailing vociferously if he would not wait. Then Jonathan and Fred became bored with her. So she took up with a 'rogue' cat, much her own age, called Timothy. This proved a disastrous alliance: complaints kept coming from neighbours.

A woman who was dyeing curtains a deep rose-pink left the dye-bath unattended outside the back door while she answered the telephone. The two cats, consumed with curiosity, began to explore. Timothy dabbled his paws into the water and when he took them out was wearing rose-coloured gloves. Sadie, losing her balance, fell into the bath and emerged a dripping, dejected, totally rose-red cat! As if that were not enough, the two then sprang into a basket of freshly washed linen ready to be hung on the clothes-line.

Another day Timothy's owner, having laid a Wilton stair-carpet, proceeded to touch up with white paint the boarding on either side, then went away to clean his brushes. He had shut Timothy in the garden, but forgotten about the cat-flap. On his return he found the precious carpet dotted with a white, daisy-like pattern.

One summer's day the local school was holding its annual examinations. The children were scribbling industriously or sighing under a teacher's scrutiny. They were also being scrutinised through the open window by four cats: Timothy, Jonathan, Fred and Sadie. A child, looking up from her desk, greeted them. Chaos ensued. The cats scrambled in, one after the other, knocking pot-plants from the window-sill, leaping on to desks, scattering paper and pens. The children screamed with delight, while the cats, diving under furniture, overturned chairs and blackboard. The teacher, cleaving the air ineffectually with a T-square, tried to drive them out. Too late. The formerly quiet classroom was turned into bedlam. The examination was called off.

6

Miscellanea

Fable and folklore

Whereas God, the lord of life, created the cat, Satan, the bringer of death, created the mouse. To destroy life once and for all, the devil's mouse proceeded to gnaw a hole in the hull of Noah's Ark, so that all the creatures on board might be destroyed. God's cat, however, killed the mouse, and a frog, having squeezed into the hole, blocked the entrance.

Tailless cats are a reminder that, according to legend, the pair of cats due to enter the Ark were late. Noah was just closing the door and in doing so nipped off their tails!

Rocks along parts of the Manx coast slope steeply and are slippery. The original cats, it has been said, found it easiest to slither down, sitting on their behinds—with the consequence that their tails were gradually worn away!

In the Khasi hills of Assam there lived a cat and a tiger. One day the tiger fell ill and began to shiver with cold. The cat, therefore, determined to bring fire to him—which entailed entering the dwelling of man, for in no place else was fire to be found. This the cat did, and carrying a burning brand in his mouth returned to the tiger. But the cat—cats miss nothing—had noticed in man's home the warm hearth, the flickering fire, a bowl of tastily cooked rice, another containing fish. 'I've found a better place to live in,' he told the tiger, and, having done what he could for his friend, he installed himself in man's home, since when there have been domestic cats in the hills of Khasi.

One day the tiger fell ill and began to shiver with cold. The cat, therefore, determined to bring fire to him . . .'

Long ago in China an emperor possessed a cat who, after rain had fallen for three days, plunged into a pool of water, was transformed into a winged dragon and flew away, never to be seen again.

One day a Siamese princess was bathing in a pool. To be sure her rings were safe she had slipped them on to the tail of her cat who, to prevent them from falling off, bent her tail—hence, to this day, the kink often seen in the tail of the Siamese.

A pair of cats in Siam were searching in the woods for a cup that had disappeared from a temple. When at last they found it, the female, with characteristic ingenuity, twisted her tail around the stem of the cup to keep it safe. Meanwhile the male went off to report the good news. By the time he returned, five kittens had been born: one and all, they had a kink in their tails.

A dark patch low on the neck of a Siamese cat is called the 'temple mark'. A god, having picked up one of the sacred cats of Siam, left upon her and her descendants the imprint of his hand.

In Madras there is a rock-carving of a cat who used to sit on the bank of the river Ganges, doing penance (so he said) for his sins. So devout did he appear that the birds and mice in the neighbourhood, duly impressed, did him honour and sought his protection. And so every day at the same hour he led them in great numbers to the river to wash away their sins . . . Then it was noticed that this was the hour at which the cat had his main meal.

Three times, despite being beaten for doing so, a young Danish girl gave a saucer of milk to a cat. In gratitude, the cat wrapped her in a cloak made from his own fur, presented her with a beautiful dress, transformed himself into a prince, and married her.

A princess, so they say in the wilds of Brittany, was threatened that the prince she was to marry would die unless, in a given time, she succeeded in spinning a specified number of balls of linen thread. The time was nearly up and still she had not finished. Then five white cats came to the rescue. Day and night their spinning wheels hummed and soon the task was completed. The spinning ceased, yet the humming went on. This was the reward given to the cats for their kindness. At the wedding of the princess the cats, decked with jewels, sat on silk cushions—purring.

An old woman in the west of Ireland was sitting by the hearth, spinning far into the night, when she heard a miaow at the door. She opened it, and a cat she had not seen before, followed by two kittens, walked in, sat down by the fire, and began to purr and to wash.

The woman was very tired and very poor. Even so, she got up, poured out a bowl of milk and put it in front of the cats, near the fire. The cat and kittens lapped up the milk and again began to purr.

Then, to the woman's astonishment, the cat spoke: 'Don't ever again sit up spinning far into the night. Trust the cats!' And at one bound cat and kittens disappeared up the chimney. The old woman noticed something glinting in the ashes on the hearth. It was a silver coin, worth more than she would earn were she to sit up spinning for many, many nights.

Cats and kings

The saying 'A cat may look at a king' is attributed to Maximilian I. The Emperor was deep in conversation with Hieronymus Resch, a maker of woodcuts, when he noticed that Resch's cat, who was lying stretched out on the table, was staring up at him with a look of deep suspicion.

According to tradition a king whose hands have been anointed and a cat whose paws have been buttered are more likely to remain where they ought to: the king in his kingdom, the cat in his home.

Cats, Manx folklore tells us, have a king of their own who, living during the day the life of the common domestic breed, at nightfall assumes regal powers and roams abroad in 'fiery splendour'. Moreover, if someone shuts out a cat at night against his will the king gives orders to the fairies to let him in.

In 1926, when the new king of Siam was crowned, a white cat was carried in the procession. The soul of the king's predecessor, it was said, was embodied in this cat.

Believe it or not . . .

A short-haired cat, accidentally shut in the refrigerated section of a ship carrying meat from New Zealand to London, arrived in good condition, having grown, on the voyage, a long, thick coat.

Dante had a cat who liked to sit supporting a lighted candle between her forepaws.

Erasmus found that on paying a visit in England he was expected to kiss his host and hostess, a bevy of girls, and the family cat.

To keep on the 'right side' of Ingres, the painter, you had to flatter Procope, his cat.

A Canadian cat who wore walnut shells on his paws became an expert ice skater.

A cat belonging to a guitar-player rushes to the instrument when hungry and begins to twang the strings.

In a bishop's palace in the west of England one of the duties of the butler is to adjust the notices on the 'in or out' board in the hall:

The Bishop	In —	Out
The Chaplain	In —	Out
The Cat	In —	Out

The poet W. B. Yeats, when he went to collect his fur coat at the Abbey Theatre, Dublin, found a cat lying on it, fast asleep. Following the example of Muhammad, he cut off a piece from the coat sooner than disturb the cat.

A cat in the Stock Exchange gained a reputation for sensing how the market was going. If he held his tail high, it was a good time to buy; if horizontal, it would be wise to sell.

If a hungry cat is shown his plate—even empty—his eyes often dilate to four or five times their normal size.

At La Paz in Bolivia in 1972 an army of two thousand cats was raised to combat a tropical fever spread by jungle rodents. When the fever abated the cats were retained in case there might be a 'come-back'.

Frederick the Great stipulated that the citizens of conquered towns should provide levies of cats to protect stores.

A female tabby killed 12,480 rats in the White City Stadium during a period of six years.

Christopher Milne (the original Christopher Robin), when appearing on 'Desert Island Discs', asked, at his wife's suggestion, to take with him as a 'luxury' a pregnant cat!

A cat does not like his hind legs to be stroked: it frightens him.

A cat of my acquaintance gobbles up breadcrumbs scattered in the grass for the birds. If offered crumbs indoors he walks away in disgust.

The R34, the first dirigible balloon to cross the Atlantic, had a cat on board, a tabby called Jazz.

A cat who had a broken leg supported by a splint, being attacked by another cat, held down his opponent with all the strength of one forepaw and used the splint to bash him!

A cat on a kibbutz in Galilee was so fond of oranges that she learned to peel them for herself.

Motherhood

The cat in general is an exemplary mother. She prepares for the birth of her kittens, suckles them, protects them, trains them and in due course, with a wisdom not always apparent in human mothers, teaches them independence, showing them how to fend for themselves. 'I've done my part,' she seems to say. 'It's up to you now.'

Dinah, in Lewis Carroll's *Through the Looking-Glass*, was a thoroughly businesslike mother. When washing her kittens she used one paw to hold them down by the ears, while with the other she rubbed their faces. A Jerusalem correspondent tells of a similarly practical approach: a mature cat helped a younger one to deliver her first kittens and was duly rewarded later when the young cat took over 'babysitting' to give the older animal, burdened with a family of her own, some time off.

Not all cats, however, have the same degree of maternal instinct. The nineteenth-century scholar and author Andrew Lang tells of two cats—one belonging to the drawing-room, the other to the kitchen—who each had a family at the same time. The drawing-room cat carried her kittens downstairs one by one, leaving them to be looked after by the common kitchen cat. She visited her offspring several times each day, seeing that all was in order.

She was still 'one up' on Mehitabel, the cat in the poems of Don Marquis, who thought of nothing but luxury and success as a film star and consequently neglected her kittens shamefully, sometimes even mislaying them entirely. Asked about one litter, she answered in surprise:

> why goodness gracious i seem to remember
> that i did have some kittens . . .

There was also the feckless white Annabelle who, indifferent to her kittens, presented them one by one to a large tabby tom belonging to Sheila Burnford, author of *The Incredible Journey*. Although he was not their father he cared for them, protected them, purred over them and finally installed them in a human household where they were made welcome and were visited by him on and off throughout each day.

When in doubt . . .

The majority of cats are extremely fastidious and wash themselves from head to tail. However, they do not do this solely for hygienic reasons. They wash also to hide embarrassment, or when confronted with a dilemma. Having mewed for a door to be opened, the cat will subsequently have second thoughts. To go through, or not to go through? And so, sooner than commit himself, he sits down in the entrance and proceeds to wash.

'When in doubt—any kind of doubt—wash.' That, says Paul Gallico's Jennie, is the golden rule.

The marriage cats

In a church in California the bride and bridegroom stood side by side in the sanctuary. A red carpet stretched the length of the church. Suddenly a white Persian cat, tail waving, began to walk up the aisle. He glanced right and left, in the direction of the guests, then went on.

In the sanctuary he made a circle around the bride, brushing her dress with his tail. Then, having walked round the bridegroom, he sat motionless, a little way off, watching the ceremony.

A black cat stood on the steps of the church.
A black cat lay in the doorway of the hotel where the reception was held.
A black cat crossed the hall of the hotel.
A black cat meandered through the room while the wedding breakfast was being served.
A black cat waited by the taxi in which bride and bridegroom left for the station.
A black cat was standing on the platform as the train drew in.

Advertisements

Wanted: A solid cat.

Dazzlingly beautiful tortie kitten, charming, intelligent, very highly strung, needs wonderful home immediately, to get away from bossy mother and four horrid red brothers.

Cat seeks post as companion. Interferes with everything. Interrupts everything. Most conscientious.

Refined home wanted for refined cat who likes to be the centre of everything.

'A tabby with whom I am acquainted . . . rolls a raw egg off the table on to the floor and laps up the yolk, leaving the white and the shell.'

On the menu

A tabby with whom I am acquainted, when an occasion presents itself, rolls a raw egg off the table on to the floor and laps up the yolk, leaving the white and the shell.

Ernest Hemingway's favourite cat liked mangoes and avocados.

Mary Shelley, wife of the poet, asked her husband one day to come into the garden to watch their cat eating a rose.

Individual cats have been known to enjoy the following:

Asparagus tips
Chocolate doughnuts
Waffles
Corn on the cob
Toffee
Mild Gruyère cheese
Soft-boiled egg
Chopped parsley

Marzipan
Peanuts
The skin of a baked potato
Orange segments
Custard skin
Cockroaches and caterpillars

Cat-flaps

A don living in Cambridge had a cat-flap made for the convenience of Jeremiah, his large, solemn black cat who—so it appeared—kept himself to himself, ignoring all neighbours, human and animal. Imagine the don's astonishment on returning one evening from London to find in his study, seated in a semi-circle facing his own cat, four feline visitors who, on his entrance, showed not the slightest embarrassment or interest. Jeremiah, as usual, remained unmoved.

Again in Cambridge, over two hundred years earlier, Sir Isaac Newton had two holes made in his door—one for his cat and a smaller one for her kittens.

In a farmhouse in Andalusia I noticed a compromise between the simple hole and the comparatively elaborate doors of today: a hole protected by a thick curtain of felt which was pushed open, in this instance, by the paw of an enormous amber-coloured cat with pale yellow, black-rimmed eyes. Somerset Maugham mentions similar cat-flaps which he saw during his travels in Andalusia.

Outsizes

Thomas O'Malley, native of Cardiff, named after the alley-cat in the film *The Aristocats*. White, with black and brown markings on head, back and tail. Weight 37 lb. Waistline 27 in. Not a gourmandiser: porridge for breakfast; at night a small tin of cat food. Brothers and sisters normal in size. Verdict of vet: 'Perfectly fit.' Rattles door-knocker when he wants to come in. Purr as loud as an electric bell. Brought home a stray kitten which he looked after as if she were his own.

Tiger, native of Billericay, Essex. Long-haired tabby and white. Weight 42 lb. Waistline 33 in. To be included in the next *Guinness Book of Records*. Disposed to be idle. Fastidious. Lover of luxury. Will eat only fresh cod and stewed steak. Abnormally shy—has been suggested he should see a psychologist. Too timid to go near a mouse; sits meekly in the garden, indifferent to birds hopping and twittering around him.

Hyacinth. Colossal cat. White except for a black 'skull-cap'. Sits on the counter in an obscure shop in an area of London that has lost its elegance but kept its character: the kind of shop that sells anything from umbrellas to gob-stoppers. 'What a *wonderful* cat!' I said. 'He deserves to have his photograph in the paper.' 'No, no,' his mistress replied, reacting like a peasant on a remote Aegean island who, hearing her child praised, fears the Evil Eye. 'No, no,' she repeated reproachfully. 'We want to keep him safe. We like him to stay in the "back" not in the shop . . . But cats won't be told!'

Some Oxford cats

At Oxford in the covered market a storekeeper put out in the evenings an empty barrel that had contained olives in oil. A bevy of cats used to assemble and lick the barrel clean.

Oxford is swarming with plump, sleek, contented cats, nibbling grass, sitting under archways, greeting passers-by, thumping on doors to be admitted to lectures, hogging the fire, 'plopping' into bedrooms, through open windows, at dead of night.

In April 1973 a scholar and cat-lover from the USA, resident at Somerville and temporarily separated from her own cat, wrote: 'I can only pat the pretty, well-loved, well-fed cats of Oxford as I pass them on my way to great libraries. I wish all cats were as happy, friendly, and secure.'

The following is an inked notice pinned on one of the doors in St Anne's College:

**- PLEASE REMEMBER
TO CLOSE THIS DOOR**

**HIS LORDSHIP FEELS
THE COLD**

Compare this with the following eighteenth-century enamel plaque on a house in Kensington:

DANGER

BEWARE OF THE CAT

Femina et felis

Ah, Cat, you are Woman,
You are the first and the last breath of love;
You filter off my red today.
You were sacred when the Walls fell down,
Now scarred you remain
The survivor of a barren earth,
A void sky.
Like woman, you arise;
Like woman, you take your bed
Among the stars.

Cathy Thomas, aged 14

In memoriam

Quae cum apud nos plus
Quam duodecim annos
Feliciter vixisset supremum
Nobis plorantibus
Infeliciter obiit.
                              AD XVIII Kal. Dec. MCMLXVI

Quis novit si spiritus filiorum Adam ascendat sursum
et si spiritus iumentorum descendat deorsum?

After living with us happily for more than twelve years, she died to
our great sorrow on 15 November 1956.

'Who knoweth if the spirit of the children of Adam ascend upward,
and if the spirit of the beasts descend downward?'   Eccles. 3:21.

In memory of SOSNA, faithful and beloved friend of all at St
Mary's Rectory, Derby, for 17 years, who departed from us on the
9th October, still remembered with affection by many.   H.W.

On earth you slipped through silken grasses in an Irish meadow,
pausing to sniff red sorrel and buttercups that dusted your ebony
face with gold. Do you now, a phantom puss, roam in Penelope's
fields of Asphodel?

7
Cats in the Church

In *Memoires d'outre-tombe* Chateaubriand tells of a large grey and red cat banded with black who had the distinction of being born in the Vatican, in the loggia of Raphael, and of being permitted to recline on a fold of the white soutane worn by Pope Leo XII.

'When the successor of St Peter died,' Chateaubriand writes, 'I inherited the bereaved animal. He is called Micetto and, furthermore, is known as "the Pope's cat"—the latter title winning for him high regard among the devout. I do all I can to alleviate his exile and help him forget the Sistine Chapel and the vast dome of Sant' Angelo where, far above the ground, he used to take his daily promenade.'

All this sounds impressive. In fact this intellectual Pope, patron of letters and lover of music, lived very simply. He and his cat enjoyed each other's company and fed on small helpings of *polenta*.

I do not know the name of the cat who belonged to Pope Pius IX. However, when the Pope dined, the cat came in at the same time as the soup. He used to spring on to a chair drawn up to the table and sit facing the Pope, silent and respectful, until the Holy Father had finished his meal. Thereupon he, too, was given his food from the hands of the Pope, after which he withdrew until the next day when the ritual was repeated.

* * *

Another ecclesiastic attached to cats was Cardinal Richelieu. He had a room fitted up as a cattery where two attendants, Abel and Tessandiers, waited on the animals, feeding them morning and evening on pâté made from the breast of chicken.

Some say that Richelieu cared only for kittens—particularly white kittens, whose antics amused him for hours on end—and that when they grew into cats he lost interest and acquired a fresh batch of kittens. This does not seem consistent, however, with the well authenticated story that in his will he left a quite considerable sum for his fourteen cats, whose names included Pyramé, Thisbe, Lucifer and Perruque—the last two having been born inside the wig of Racan the academician. Furthermore, he left a bequest for a commonplace cat much loved by a widow to whom he had given financial help.

* * *

Of Cardinal Wolsey there has come down the sinister story that, while stroking his cat with one hand, he would nonchalantly sign a death warrant with the other.

* * *

Lady Morgan, who visited at Naples the much loved Monsignore Capecelatro, formerly Bishop of Taranto, wrote in her *Book of the Boudoir* (1829) of his passion for cats—*passione gattesco*. He would not allow cats to be excluded from the dining-room: his guest, he assured her, would find them delightful company.

Between the first and second courses, Lady Morgan relates, the door opened and in came several enormous Angoras who were introduced as Pantalone, Desdemona, Otello, and other such distinguished names. Having taken their places on chairs by the table they sat quiet and motionless. When the Bishop asked one of his chaplains to serve the Signora Desdemona, the butler, stepping forward, said: 'My Lord, the Signora will prefer to wait for the roasts!'

Sir Henry Holland, Queen Victoria's physician, used to talk of a 'magnificent cat' belonging to the household of 'this venerable and kind-hearted prelate'.

Moreover an epitaph written in honour of the cat Pantalone contains the lines:

> Il mourut aimé tendrement
> D'un maître que tout le monde aime.
>
> He died tenderly beloved
> Of a master whom all the world loves.

* * *

There are, of course, ecclesiastical cats of a less exalted station. George Borrow in *Wild Wales* tells of the cat of Llangollen, who was either left behind or chose to remain when an Anglican vicar moved from the district. The vicar having gone, the inhabitants of that neighbourhood, who were almost all dissenters, proceeded to torment the cat, because, being associated with the Church of England, he deserved in their view only the worst treatment. Although they showed no enmity to other cats they hurled abuse at this one and even threw sticks and stones at him. Moved with compassion, George Borrow acquired the animal, fed him, cared for him, and cured him of a skin infection, until he turned into a fine cat with a smooth, sleek coat.

Before leaving the neighbourhood Borrow found a home for him with a young woman of 'sound Church principles', where he lived content and unmolested until one day he suddenly 'sprang up from the hearth into the air and died'.

* * *

The following account of a feline 'dynasty' was written for me by a canon-residentiary of a cathedral in the Low Countries. He has exceptional ease in forming a rapport with a cat, even on the shortest acquaintance. One day a highly nervous blue Persian, born in the Congo, jumped on to the canon's lap immediately on being introduced, then clambered on to his shoulder, where she lay for over an hour. She had never given this token of affection even to her owners.

Between the years 1919 and 1968 there was in my home a dynasty of four cats and, in addition, an 'assistant' who dealt with such mundane matters as killing mice. The first assistant, a beautiful cat with short grey fur and light green eyes, was somewhat wild and unsociable by disposition. Believed to be female, he was named Jeanette, and subsequently, having turned out to be male, kept the name.

The first two cats of the dynasty were called Pilous—Pilous I, then Pilous II. A strange name of no apparent significance, but it sounded well!

They were ordinary striped tabbies, well loved by our entire family. My father, who respected and esteemed them, used to stroke their silky coats and pull their tails, while singing in English 'poor old Pilous', to the tune of 'Three Blind Mice'. He was not, however, as crazy as the rest of us, who at mealtimes kept peering under the dining-room table to see what Pilous was up to—that is, if he was not in his favourite place; for normally (I am thinking for the moment of Pilous II) he used to sit between my mother and the back of her chair.

Sometimes, to make his presence known, he would tap my mother's arm or that of her neighbour in the hope of being offered some morsel. One day a member of the Senate, the Duke of Ursel, came to lunch and received similar attentions, which he did not seem to appreciate!

Among the many qualities of Pilous I was a sense of justice. He was seen one day sharing with the assistant, Jeanette, a large fish skin, which he divided into two halves with his paw.

Neither Pilous I nor Pilous II liked our going on holiday. For a few days after our return they made their displeasure known—even to the extent of spitting at us. Then, having vented their wrath, they calmed down and reverted to their normal selves.

Both these cats lived to the age of sixteen.

Our next cat, Caligula, had quite a long black coat without a trace of white; golden eyes, and a feather-like tail. He was a sort of political refugee: that is to say, he first of all lived with my niece whose home was on the far side of our garden wall. She, however, had two large dogs, a Great Dane and a Labrador, kind but slightly patronising animals—somewhat rough companions for the kitten that Caligula then was. Therefore, choosing freedom, he crossed the 'stone curtain' and sought asylum with us: an arrangement acceptable on both sides of the wall.

Caligula had a sense of humour. He liked to spring out of a dark corner on to the feet of passers-by. In the night he used to push open the half-closed door of my room, jump on to my bed and flatten himself down between the blankets so that only whiskers and the tip of a tail were visible.

During meals he sat on a chair, his front paws resting on the table. He lost his composure only when there was fish or liver. He also liked cake—especially Dundee cake. He would nibble a piece of lettuce leaf if it were offered him, probably out of politeness. Devoted to my mother, who was now growing old, he would sit on her lap for hours.

When my mother died at our home on the coast and the coffin was brought to our town house and placed in one of the salons, the cat, showing considerable agitation, tried to come into the room. Not allowed to do so, he disappeared, and returned later carrying in his mouth a dead bird. This he laid respectfully outside the door of the salon: a tribute to one whom he had loved.

In 1959 an incident occurred that had something in common with this. I was away from home for two months, during which time Caligula used to roam from room to room in search of me. On my return he gave me a tremendous welcome, then disappeared. After an hour he came back with a bird in his mouth, jumped on to my desk and put it down on the blotting paper.

Possibly his greatest achievement was his defence of a maid of ours who used to look after him. She was gathering herbs in the garden when a dog, known for its viciousness, jumped over the wall and began to rush at her. Caligula, fur standing on end, claws bared, flew at the dog which, its muzzle badly mauled, gave a great howl and fled back the way it had come.

Caligula had grown old. He no longer played his tricks or chased falling leaves in graceful leaps and turns. When I worked in the garden he sat quietly watching me. Then one day, when we were there together, he came up to me and brushed his tail against my legs. I did not know that this was his farewell.

The next morning he was found dead in the scullery. Our housekeeper, in tears, buried him. She put a small wooden cross on his grave.

Caligula's death left an aching void. Asked one day how things were going, I replied: 'I'm mourning the death of a dear cat.' I did not want, another, I felt.

Then the unexpected happened. I was offered the gift of a blue Persian kitten: a little pedigree cat with whose lineage not even the Shah of Persia could vie. When I opened the small cardboard box in which he was brought, and scratched his tiny head, he began to purr. Then I let him loose in the kitchen where, in true feline fashion, he proceeded to examine everything. We called him Caligula II.

A prince among cats, he ate princely food: the best of raw beef, with yeast powder and flaked carrot. Later, he ate six ounces a day of the finest quality meat. If it was not of the finest quality, or not perfectly fresh, he would not touch it. He did not drink much milk. If he wanted some, he would stand by the refrigerator and give a tap with his paw. If, when the milk was poured out, he wanted it warmed, he would go to the gas stove and again tap. During meals he used to sit on a chair beside mine, always dignified. He rarely accepted food at the table, but he liked the dining-room: the shining silver and the mirrors in which I saw him, many times, looking at himself.

He caught a mouse only once. It was to 'prove' himself: he did not eat it. Unlike most cats, he did not pounce on birds and kill them. If he came upon a fledgling fallen from its nest, he would carry it gently into the kitchen, as if to be cared for.

His toys included a little motor-car, some pheasants' legs and a rubber ball. He would chase the ball at an incredible speed, leap into the air five times his own height. Each night at 10.30 he assembled his playthings in a corner of the kitchen, jumped on to the table and lay stretched full length on a newspaper, waiting to be brushed. If he was not at once attended to, he protested with loud mews.

He liked heights: the top of a ladder or the top of a cupboard. When he was young he had several falls, slipping on the polished furniture. Later, he learnt to measure heights and could land with precision, like a bird.

He showed remarkable tact, indeed a sense of occasion. One day when, as Chaplain of the Forces, I had invited to a formal lunch some generals and other high-ranking officers, Caligula behaved impeccably. On the arrival of my guests, he walked in, dignified, poised, his feathery tail held high, and made straight for the two most important of my visitors, greeted them with a sweep of his tail, then withdrew.

Usually at the end of meals, before returning to my study, I would ask him whether he was coming with me or not. The answer was an unmistakable *oui* or *rien*. When I used my typewriter he would jump on to the table and play with my pencils, pushing them one after another on to the floor. He liked to move the keys of the typewriter with one paw, while with the other he tried to 'catch' the letter.

Sometimes on Sunday I would spread a blue blanket over my knees. Caligula would jump up and, purring contentedly, remain there for hours at a time while I was reading.

His preferences in music were remarkable. One day I was listening to a concert of classical music on the radio, while he slept in an armchair—the best armchair! When the orchestra played Mozart he woke, jumped down from the chair and lay full length in front of the loudspeaker, his head slightly inclined in the direction of the music. When the Mozart ended he went back to his chair. After this I experimented with my record player, choosing, among other compositions, some of Mozart's symphonies. Caligula's reaction was the same.

His amusing ways and demonstrations of affection were for me exclusively. By disposition he was a shy cat and, in the company of strangers, reserved.

My housekeeper was becoming old, and was in bad health. In 1968 she had to go into a nursing home. At that time, too, I had to be much away from home, and Caligula was a cat who needed human companionship. After much thought, therefore, I decided to give him as a present to a cousin of mine, a woman who loved and understood cats. There was another cat in the household, a 'commoner'. Surprisingly, this presented difficulties on neither side. The two accepted each other from the beginning, without rivalry or contention. But the relationship between the princely blue Persian and the 'commoner' was defined by and dependent upon prestige, as between master and servant. Caligula ate his meals first, the other cat waiting for his, respectfully, at a distance.

In giving Caligula away I had done what seemed best for him. He was well cared for and became attached to his new owner. Nevertheless he did not forgive me for having betrayed, as he understood it, his exclusive devotion to me.

He is dead now.

I shall remember always the joy and tender love bestowed upon me by this beautiful creature of God, who showed a fidelity surpassing that of many a human being.

* * *

The tabby (she was always known as 'Cat') was less than eight weeks old when she came to the Carmelite Priory in Kensington: so small was she that she barely filled the palm of the monk's hand outstretched to welcome her. It was hard to believe that a purr so loud could come from so small a creature.

The offspring of a country cat used to roaming fields and woods on the outskirts of Oxford, she had inherited something of her mother's courageous, independent spirit. Despite being so small that there was a risk of her being trodden underfoot or caught in a door, she soon familiarised herself with the geography of the building. Her grey-blue eyes shining, her little tail held high, she found her way along corridors, up and down staircases, into the refectory, the sacristy, the library, parlours, church—full of curiosity, purring with contentment. Having learnt to clamber on to the lower shelf of a trolley used to carry cutlery, she allowed herself to be conveyed from the kitchen to the refectory.

As the months passed she grew from kitten to cat—not a large cat, but well built and healthy, her sleek coat marked with clearly defined black stripes.

She had a sense of fun. In the late evening she would dart into the sacristy, where the vestments were laid out in readiness for the Masses in the morning, reach up with a paw, dab at a chasuble and bring it slithering down on to the floor . . . then another one!

In the garden she sharpened her claws on the trunks of trees, sniffed flowers, nibbled blades of grass, climbed branches, peered through foliage. She had a companion: a large tame rabbit. They accepted each other, and sat on the same wooden seat—the cat at one end, the rabbit at the other. Or on warm days they lay in the shade of a castor-oil plant, the cat resting against the rabbit as though reclining on a sofa.

Cat maintained her independence. Even when she had young kittens she would go off on her own, nobody knew where. Meanwhile the rabbit used to escort the kittens into her burrow, where the cat, on her return, would join them.

Homes were found for four out of the six kittens. The remaining two were kept in the priory. After they had grown into cats, the mother disappeared. Why she did so is a mystery. She was seen from time to time in the neighbourhood, looking in fine fettle. Had she been lured away? This is possible, for the rabbit disappeared

'The two young cats were known as the Brother and the Sister. Both tabbies, they differed quite considerably.'

at almost the same time. Or did the cat, resenting attention paid to her offspring, revert to her mother's roaming habits?

The two young cats were known as the Brother and the Sister. Both tabbies, they differed quite considerably. The Brother's coat was striped, the Sister's mainly spotted, and thicker in texture than his. He cared for his passably well; she took pride in hers, constantly washed it and puffed it out so that the fur looked longer than it was. Her paws were bigger than his; so was her tail. She was indeed a fine cat, always spruce, whereas a torn ear gave the Brother a somewhat rakish look.

Their voices also differed. He would give an occasional miaow, to show he wanted something or to convey approval or disapproval. She kept up a continual conversation composed of little cooing notes, talking to herself as she picked her way along a window-ledge or trotted the length of a passage. The Brother was a great cat for using the telephone: he would purr and mew loudly into the mouthpiece, and enjoyed dialling numbers with his paw.

The two had different tastes in food. The Brother liked a particular brand of cat food, and would open the packet with his paws, then thrust his head inside. He also liked toasted crusts: he would sit in the kitchen in front of a drawer in which these were kept, waiting for it to be opened. The Sister liked large solid bones. When she had stripped off and eaten the meat she would carry the bones, one at a time, and put them inside a box lined with paper in which the Brother liked to lie, thus making it impossible for him to do so. This problem was solved when one of the monks built him a house of his own, like a dog-kennel in shape, at right-angles to the priory wall, standing a few inches above the ground and sheltered from the wind. It was lined with carpeting which was shaken each day. Only the Brother went into this house. On fine days he would sit just inside, his paws tucked under him, his yellow eyes blinking in the sunshine.

The two cats were devoted to each other. If one disappeared the other went around mewing desolately. They could, however, become suddenly jealous. Then yowls rang out and fur flew.

They were particularly attached to the monk who had made the Brother's house. Whenever he went away they were restless for days beforehand and, when his luggage appeared in the hall, viewed it with baleful looks. On his return they either ignored him or—there is no knowing what a cat will do—welcomed him with purrs and mews. On one occasion when he had come out of hospital and liked to sit reading a book in the garden, they made this impossible by scrambling over him, thrusting their heads against him, kneading with their claws and turning over the pages with a paw.

One morning when this same priest was coming into church vested to say Mass, the Brother, appearing as if from nowhere, preceded him like an acolyte. This cat had an extraordinary sense of time. For a while I was doing research in one of the parlours on Saturday evenings, using books belonging to the priory library. Without fail, the Brother arrived at seven o'clock, observing always the same ritual. He would race along the corridor, pause for a moment, always at the same spot, scratch the matting with his claws, then dash on as if the act of scratching had given him renewed vigour. Then he would lie curled on the table, sleeping or peering from time to time through half-closed lids. Now and again voices or footsteps were audible in the passage. Usually he took no notice, but occasionally he would sit bolt upright. That meant his monastic 'friend' was on the way. I had heard nothing, but the cat knew.

As nine o'clock approached another routine was observed. The Brother would leap to the floor, ask to be let out, trot along the corridor (no scraping of the carpet this time), then disappear down a flight of steps to the parish club, where he mingled among the visitors, enjoying a morsel of cake or a sandwich. The Sister did not attend the club. Her diversion was a catechism class held for children on Saturday mornings. People called her the 'unsociable' cat. She was not unsociable, but shy, and the company of the children dispelled the shyness.

* * *

At the Teresianum, the Carmelite college in Rome, there used to be an enormous, formidable tabby, devoted to an old Basque brother who was both gardener and cellarer. While the old man worked in the garden, wearing a large straw hat, the cat would sit close by, watching. If the dog ventured near, the cat glowered at him so savagely that the dog was cowed and took himself off. When the dog retired to his kennel to enjoy a siesta he would often find the cat already installed, staring insolently from the entrance.

Sometimes there were rats in the cellar, but the cat disposed of these. Having killed them in a businesslike manner he pitched them disdainfully, one after another, from the cellar floor to the top step leading out of the door.

* * *

There were for a long time three black and white cats—a father and two sons—attached to the church of St Mary Abbots, Kensington.

When an organ builder to whom they had belonged left the neighbourhood, they installed themselves outside the church, attracted by the warmth of the paving stones which were heated by boilers below. A kindly verger, Mr Reginald Racher, gave them food and drink.

The saga with which I am concerned began one icy morning when the vicar, the late Prebendary Eley (subsequently Bishop of Gibraltar), arriving to take early service, found one of the cats lying stretched out, stiff with cold, on the pavement. The boilers below had failed, and the cat appeared to be dead. Indeed, he would have died if the vicar had not taken him indoors and fed him with tea-spoonfuls of egg whipped up with brandy.

Restored to health, the cat was given the name Thomas Aquinas. His brother, because he was of a somewhat timid disposition, was called Thomas Didymus: it was only after some time that this cat ventured inside the church, but having done so he made himself at home. The father, who was named Thomas Kempis, never went into the church. The verger built him a house outside and saw that he was fed and cared for.

St Mary Abbots church was infested with mice: they even nibbled the candle-wax in the sanctuary. Thomas Aquinas and Thomas Didymus put this to rights. They smelt the mice and heard them scampering below a grille in the floor, above the furnace. Sometimes they could see a mouse through the bars of the grille, but were unable to get at it. Eventually they contrived to find a way down. The slaughter was on a vast scale. Yet out of all those mice the cats not only spared one, but made a friend of him. This mouse used to be fed on cake and biscuits in the vestry, in the company of the cats, and when the verger was serving in the sanctuary he would see the mouse sitting up, a yard or so away.

Nor was it unusual during service for one cat or both to sit respectfully in the sanctuary. Or they might choose a position from which they could look up at the royal pew—at Princess Alice, Princess Marina, or Princess Margaret.

On Thursdays at 11.30 am a Communion service was held in the chapel of St Paul: because there were no steps it was convenient for elderly persons. Among those who attended was a Miss Bell who was particularly fond of the cats. Each Thursday, on their own initiative, the two cats used to take up their positions one at each end of the pew in which Miss Bell sat. While she went to the altar they remained behind with perfect decorum.

When Miss Bell died the cats met the coffin, walked ahead of it up the cloister that leads into the church, and, when it was placed on trestles and covered with a pall, sat underneath, remaining there through the night. Next morning, as the cortège moved down the aisle, the cats were sitting on the radiators to either side of the door.

The cats participated fully in the life of the church. At a baptism they would move among the people, giving particular pleasure to the children. At weddings, Thomas Aquinas had a way of sidling between the bride-to-be and her father as they went up the aisle. Then the two cats would slip away and appear again outside on the pavement among the guests, when the bride and bridegroom were getting into their car.

Over the Christmas period they sat in the crib, in the hay, eyes glinting. A child was heard to exclaim: 'Why! they're *real* animals!' For days the cats' fur smelt of hay. Parishioners brought them Christmas gifts: packets of cat's food—even a small roast chicken!

Inevitably there were those who objected to cats in a church. For a while an effort was made to discourage the Thomas brothers, but it was a half-hearted gesture. Most of the congregation liked them.

Besides, they were not in church all the time. Thomas Aquinas used to take himself off to Peter's Eating House, which was close to the entrance of St Mary Abbots, where he was made much of and fed on steak. Or he would cross Church Street—looking to right and to left—to the 'Prince of Wales', where he enjoyed a sip of beer. The proprietor threatened one day that he would have to send in a bill to cover Thomas's drinks!

One of the verger's tasks was to count the collection. He did this in the vestry, arranging the coins in neat piles: coppers, sixpences, shillings, florins and so on. Thomas Aquinas and Thomas Didymus would sit on the table watching. Then suddenly out would come a paw, scattering the coins like a child overturning a tower of bricks!

The pulpit was a forbidden area. One day the congregation was waiting for the service to begin, the loudspeaker set for a visiting preacher, when a rhythmic sound began to fill the church—growing to a crescendo, then abating, only to increase again. People did not know what to think. Then the verger had his suspicions. Sure enough, Thomas Aquinas had found his way into the pulpit and was purring full strength into the microphone.

* * *

Certain of St Philip Neri's biographers, who ought to know better, say that he made his cat an excuse for mortifying others by sending them backwards and forwards to attend upon the animal. Possibly for some of them it was mortification, but the saint's motive was surely the welfare of his pet.

Loving, as he did, the world of nature, this warm-hearted, humorous, extremely eccentric but wholly delightful founder of the Congregation of the Oratory was, not surprisingly, devoted to his cat, who, he tells us, smelt of musk. More than that: he was, to quote the mystic and writer Evelyn Underhill, 'very sound on cats'. He understood their disposition.

This being so, when the Congregation moved, in Rome, from San Girolamo della Carità to the Vallicella, he not only kept on his room at San Girolamo, so much did he like it, but, appreciating that cats become attached to their surroundings, arranged for his cat to stay on undisturbed. He was constantly going to and fro from one place to the other. If, however, he could not himself be with the cat, he sent one of his brethren to attend to her needs.

This was no mere matter of routine. The saint was full of concern. When his 'emissary' returned from San Girolamo to the Vallicella, Philip would make detailed enquiries as to the cat, regardless of who might be present, be it cardinals or other persons of distinction. 'How did you find my dear puss?' he would ask. 'You took her a tasty dinner, I hope? Is she well? Did she seem contented and comfortable? What about her appetite?'

Sometimes Philip would organise an expedition into the country outside Rome or to see the sights of the city. From time to time a mewing would be heard: it was the cat in a basket.

When the cat died in 1588, some seven years before his master, Antonio Gallonio, one of the Congregation, was mentioned, in a somewhat ironical letter of condolence, as having faithfully carried food to her 'both morning and evening'.

* * *

In London, at Brompton Oratory, St Philip Neri's twentieth-century sons have two fine cats worthy of their founder.

My first impression was of four yellow eyes peering at me suspiciously from under the table. I don't think the cats were any too pleased to see me; after all, my visit was an intrusion on their liberty, for Father Barrett-Lennard, understanding the unpredictability of cats, had kindly arranged for them to be present in one of the parlours to meet me.

Eventually they emerged, a delightful pair: one black and white, the other an attractively marked tortoiseshell, their coats shining as if polished, their movements lithe and graceful. Fortunate cats, they roam the house at will, visit the room of some honoured father, enjoy the freedom of the garden.

From the hall a staircase leads up to a landing where there hangs a drawing showing the late Father John Eveleigh Woodruff, and, sitting at his side, his large grey cat Pippo.

* * *

Another distinguished Oratorian who appreciated cats was Cardinal Newman.

To satisfy an importunate lady who insisted he should write in her album, he composed some verses about a pair of kittens. Somewhat moralistic—verging, perhaps, on the sentimental—the verses are characteristically Victorian. Yet there is a charm and discernment in this portrayal of two little cats—one pretty, the other clever—who, friendly though they are, keep, as cats do, their 'distance':

> No answer came from either cat
> But passive unconcern.

* * *

In Exeter Cathedral, at the top of a pillar in the chapel of St James, is a carving made in 1950 during the restorations after the bombing in World War II, representing the head of Tom, the cat who belonged to the chief verger. While killing a rat, Tom was attacked by an owl, and in consequence lost an eye.

This same cat used to come trotting up to a child who attended the cathedral from time to time with her father, and settle down on a chair at her side. The child, asked one day what she thought God was like, replied: 'God? Oh, she's a cat!' In later life she entered a Russian Orthodox convent where she took the name Sister Seraphim, founded a refuge for animals at Tucson, Arizona, and wrote a book about the many creatures she cared for.

In the north transept of the cathedral there is a round hole at the foot of the door opening into the clock chamber. Bishop Cotton, at Exeter from 1595 to 1621, is said to have had the hole cut for the convenience of the cathedral cat.

* * *

One day a somewhat formidable-looking tabby appeared in the church of St Mary Redcliffe, Bristol. When Mr Eli Richards, the verger, put him outside, the cat refused to leave the porch. At that point Canon Bateman Champain, who was coming in, said: 'Let him stay.'

And stay he did. He used to wait for the organist, jump on to his lap and sit there while he played. He was also devoted to the verger and to his son Edward. When this cat died, permission was given to bury him in the churchyard. An impressive headstone bears the words 'The Church Cat 1912–1927'.

* * *

The ancient Book of Lismore, an Irish collection of legends of the saints, tells of three young clerics who determined to sail the seas and spread the Gospel. Putting their whole trust in God, they agreed to take nothing with them save three loaves.

Then, at the last minute, the youngest of the three changed his mind. 'I'll take the little cat, after all,' he said.

8
The language of the cat

The cat's means of communication include voice, silence, movement, and facial expression—sometimes one at a time, sometimes
one complementing another.

The Cheshire Cat replies politely and good-naturedly to the
bewildered questions of Alice, while he sits by the fireside or on the
branch of a tree, grinning from ear to ear—the grin signifying
contentment, self-assurance, perspicacity. When, however, he is
told by the king that he may kiss the royal hand, that is quite
another matter; he retorts drily: 'I'd rather not!' As to the queen's
peremptory 'Off with his head!'—her words are a waste of breath.
The cat, instead of showing fear or indignation, simply vanishes with

'The cat, instead of showing fear or indignation, simply vanishes with
disarming suddenness. Only the grin remains . . .'

disarming suddenness. Only the grin remains . . . and even the grin is fading. The Cheshire Cat is acceptable—human language and all —because Lewis Carroll understands, as far as anyone can, the feline personality.

Another talking cat who carries conviction is Saki's Tobermory, from *The Chronicles of Clovis*, who epitomises not only conversational cats but also feline superiority in the face of human folly, meanness and deception. It would be difficult to think of anything more scathing than Tobermory's reply to Lady Blemley's faltering attempt to apologise for spilling his milk on the drawing-room carpet: 'After all, it's not *my* Axminster!' Or his retort to Sir Wilfrid's hearty efforts to avoid his acid tongue by banishing him to the kitchen on the pretext of an extra meal. 'Possibly,' Tobermory concedes, 'cats have nine lives, but they have only *one* liver.' Yes, a cat of the calibre of Tobermory can make a human feel very small.

Acceptable, too, is the centuries-old story of the abbot of a Buddhist monastery who was shooing away some doves when a cat, watching what was happening, was heard to say in a loud voice: 'What a pity!' The abbot, disconcerted and alarmed, rebuked the cat, threatening to drive him away, even kill him. Then the cat spoke a second time, explaining, in some detail, the circumstances in which animals are able to converse with humans. The abbot, impressed, told the cat that, after all, he might remain in the monastery. Whereupon the cat—for you can't get round a cat just at your convenience!—gave three ceremonial bows, departed, and was not seen again.

In 1875 a woman living in Toulon claimed that she owned a talking cat whose advice she always sought and followed. This cat, when death was approaching, expressed a wish to be given a 'decent' burial. Not daring to inter him in the churchyard, his owner did the next best thing: she buried him against the wall of the church tower, commending his soul to God.

Stéphane Mallarmé, the story goes, lying awake one night listening to the cats outside, heard one say to another: 'What are you doing these days?' to which the first replied: 'Just now I'm pretending I'm the Mallarmés' cat!' And in Ludwig Tieck's play *Der Gestiefelte Kater* (Puss in Boots, 1797), Kater Heinze, the tom, makes the observation: 'We cats are all capable of talking had we not acquired from living with human beings a contempt for speech.'

In his *Historie of Foure-Footed Beastes* (1607) Edward Topsell notes that the cat has a variety of sounds by which she makes known her wants: 'She whisketh with her voyce to beg and complain, another time to testify her delight and pleasure.' Paul de Kock, too, says that cats have different miaows for different purposes— *miaulements particuliers pour chaque chose.* Montaigne has no doubt as to their ability to 'talk and reason with one another'. James, the cat belonging to Canon Reginald Cant, Chancellor of York Minster, was a great talker, skilfully catching the cadence of voices. He and the Canon's housekeeper carried on long conversations. James also expected to participate in committee meetings, and if ignored would knock over the waste-paper basket and get inside.

Andrew Lang notices the language a mother cat reserves for her kittens: 'a soft trilling sound . . . a pure caress of tone'. When kittens belonging to my cat Jemima were, on one occasion, born dead, she went about the house crying piteously, insisting that cupboards and wardrobes should be opened, lids removed from boxes. Then, when all hope had to be abandoned, she continued to dream of her young, making as she did so little caressing, cooing sounds and reaching out her paws as if to clasp her kittens.

Charles Darwin, in *Expression of Emotion*, writes: 'Cats use their voices much as a means of expression, and they utter under various emotions and desires, at least six or seven sounds. The purr of satisfaction, which is made both during inspiration and expiration, is one of the most curious.' In *Through the Looking-Glass* Alice remarks somewhat petulantly that whatever you say to kittens they always purr. Kittens, it appears, generally purr in a monotone, adult cats on two or sometimes three notes. The common French word for 'purr' is *ronron*; the nineteenth-century author Madame Michelet, however, in *Les Chats*, distinguishes a variety of notes which include *mourrons, monrons, mou-ous* and *mrrs*.

The abbé Galiani claims to discern twenty distinct mewing sounds constituting a vocabulary through which, using different combinations, the cat makes known her reactions. Champfleury says he can count sixty-three notes, although he admits that it took long practice to be able to distinguish one from another. Brian Vesey-Fitzgerald comments on the cat's 'enormous' vocabulary: it is larger, he says, than that of any mammal other than man, with the possible exception of certain monkeys.

As to caterwauling, reactions can be strong. Some people are infuriated, frenzied; others intrigued, charmed, amused. Personally I find it more than a diversion—a privilege, to be permitted to listen in the dead of night to this weird concatenation of notes, this unique concert, this music of love. Brian Vesey-Fitzgerald is indeed right to call it a 'form of song'.

F. A. Paradis de Moncrif in *Des Chats* (1728), dismissing, justifiably I think, the contention that cats are unable to sing, makes the point—easily overlooked—that an apparent dissonance can indicate not necessarily an absence of music but rather unfamiliarity, on the part of the listener, with a particular form of music. Modern music, he argues, being limited to particular divisions of sounds which we call tones and semi-tones, we are conditioned to suppose that this can alone legitimately be called music; we therefore presume to exclude voices of cats, as well as other sounds—the intervals and relations of which may be admirable—simply because they go beyond our limited experience. He reminds us that the music of the peoples of Asia can appear absurd to us, while ours makes no sense to them. Cicero says that we are all of us deaf to languages with which we are unfamiliar. Putting it differently, we could say that we hear only 'miaows' if we do not understand a language—that we sound like cats to one another.

Moncrif, who includes in his book an engraving showing a cat holding a sistrum, may be right in his belief that cats in Egypt were not only admitted to banquets, but sang at them to the accompaniment of the sistrum. In our own day Stevie Smith writes charmingly, in 'Not Waving but Drowning', of a cat in a railway train:

> Behold
> The Cat, the Cat that singeth.

And Russian folklore has an engaging story of a cat who sits on top of a golden pillar, in a remote region of the country, telling stories and singing ballads to all who care to listen.

True, there are cats—some of them highly bred Persians—who scarcely utter a sound; who open their mouths pathetically, then close them, as if they had lost their voice. At the opposite extreme are the Siamese. In range and volume of sound they surpass all other cats, yowling rather than mewing, speaking not only to express a need but as if to make some observation. At shows their voices ring out in blood-curdling protesting yells, while other cats sleep or observe a philosophic silence. Some Siamese talk more than others, but they all talk. At the first cat show held in England, in July 1871, Siamese were included ... 'an unnatural nightmare kind of cat', the *Graphic* commented.

As to the nursery rhyme about the cat and the fiddle, the association goes far back. On a medieval manuscript in the British Museum a cat is shown standing on his hind legs playing a fiddle. On a misericord in Wells Cathedral a cat plays a stringed instrument, and one on a choir-stall in Beverley Minster is playing a viol. Then there is Ted Hughes's story of a farm cat who is so efficient a mouser that every night, having finished his task in double-quick time, he can play his fiddle for hours on end. Other cats in the neighbourhood take up the idea, and a cats' orchestra is formed which assembles in a spinney and plays until dawn; then the cats hang their fiddles on the larch trees, dash home to have a meal, and sleep through the day.

I recall as a child at school practising on winter evenings in one of what were known as 'the cells'—small rooms each containing a chipped upright piano, a stool, and a spluttering gas-jet.

But in what I used to call 'my' cell there was something more: a large white cat, with a thick coat, whom I would find waiting outside on the staircase. He would jump on to the top of the piano and, while I practised scales, sit motionless as if listening intently. My attempts to play a Chopin prelude elicited a different reaction. He would cock his head, look around, make sudden dabs with a paw as if in an effort to catch something afloat upon the air. When I ceased to play, then it was his turn. He would walk up and down the keyboard, pawing the notes tentatively as though trying out the phrasing of a cadence.

Yes, cats enjoy making music. A young man employed in a restaurant had stayed on late into the night to finish clearing up. Suddenly, in the silence, he was aware of the notes of a piano coming from a room overhead. He went upstairs, somewhat tentatively—to find the restaurant cat, whose existence he had temporarily forgotten, picking her way along the keyboard.

* * *

'Silence', Richard Austin writes,

> Should be alert as cats are, curled
> Before a fire, who note within the flame the flash
> Of scarlet fin or eyes as amber as their own.

The silence of the cat is indeed alert, pregnant. It is not the mere absence of sound: it complements sound as light complements darkness, stillness movement. It can do more: it can predominate over sound. A cat can sit as if meditating like a yogi. There is, it is true, such a thing as an angry silence: baleful feline eyes, expressive of displeasure. Usually, however, the silent cat is the contented cat, the silence broken, if at all, by a gentle mew or a soothing rhythmic purr which does not intrude any more than does the whisper of wind upon the silence of the countryside.

The silence of the cat can be impressive. Ewart Milne evokes this in his little shaped poem 'Diamond cut Diamond', about two cats: 'he' in a wych-elm tree, 'she' under the tree; he looking at the clouds, she at the tree. T. S. Eliot suggests that a cat rapt in meditation is thinking about his name—not the one by which he is commonly known, but a private, 'ineffable', 'inscrutable' name, as much a secret as the hundred and ninety-ninth name of Muhammad, known only to the camel.

The cat's walk is silent: he walks on padded toes. He stalks silently, crouches silently, his eyes not for a moment averted from his prey. If, while crouching in readiness to spring, he senses that he is being watched by another cat, he is likely to straighten himself up as though he were no longer interested: cats dislike busybodies.

His spine is so constructed that, if he is in the humour to be stroked, he can silently arch his back into a bow-shaped curve— arch it so high to meet your hand that, as Rosalie Moore says in her poem 'Catalogue', there is room underneath for a 'large pumpkin'. An arched spine, however, can also indicate hostility or fear.

When two cats meet face to face it is not unusual for them to stop for a moment to greet each other, nose to nose, kiss in silence, like grand panjandrums, then continue on their ways. If by chance they are hostile the silence will assume a different quality. The two will stand stock still, facing each other, legs stiff as ramrods—a silent confrontation which will either peter out, the two parting disdainfully, or else end in a violent conflict accompanied by growls, hisses, spits, yowls, caterwauling, that accentuate the silence before and after.

In general a devotee of silence, the cat dislikes discordant voices. H. G. Wells had a cat who, if guests spoke too loudly, jumped on to the floor and made for the door. When my brother and his under-graduate friends began to argue excitedly, our cat Romulus would spring on to the window-sill and tap the pane of glass with his paw as a sign that he wanted to be let out. Madame Michelet tells how, if she sang in an exaggerated manner the high note in Schubert's 'Serenade', her cat showed displeasure by pressing two paws against her lips. A cat I know in a block of flats, if disturbed by a neighbouring party, whimpers, buries her head in her owner's lap, or covers her ears with her paws.

Writing of cats prowling silently in Trajan's Forum in Rome, Carel Capek, the Czech dramatist, notes that they ignore one another. Several sit on the same column, back to back, nervously flicking their tails, as if to indicate the difficulty of tolerating 'the presence of the slattern behind'. They have nothing, he continues, to say to each other: at best they put up with one another, in 'a scornful, negative silence'.

* * *

If the movement of a cat takes the form of what Cecil Day Lewis calls a 'consequential trot', this means he has a clear-cut purpose in mind and should on no account be distracted. If, on the other hand, he engages in what the same poet calls a 'frantic tarantella', he is thoroughly excited—probably pleasantly so. When wind is blowing or is on the way, it is not unusual for a cat to dash about wildly, not only in the garden—climbing trees, chasing leaves—but also in-doors—tearing from room to room, along passages, up and down the staircase, mats flying.

On the other hand, to be shouted at or chased (unless the chase is part of a game), or, when asleep in the garden, to be disturbed by an apple thudding to the ground—that is another matter. Again the cat dashes away, but this time in alarm. Real terror has a different effect: it causes the cat's pads to break into a sweat.

Cats can leap to surprising heights. They leap to escape danger;

to pursue a bird or insect; to join another cat on the tiles; to catch a leaf floating on the air. They do so with a sinuous grace which A. S. J. Tessimond captured to perfection:

> Cats no less liquid than their shadows
> Offer no angles to the wind.

Or a cat may choose to occupy a position—on a wall or cupboard or tree—from which, in a mood of detached superiority, he can look down upon the scene below.

This, I believe, is the motive of Poncho, a partly Polish cat of my acquaintance. *Puncio, punie* ... ('Poncho, dear Poncho ...') her master says to her in caressing tones: Poncho, with her large, wide-open eyes that have a perpetual expression of wonderment, as if she were viewing the world on the day of creation.

But Poncho has another motive: to lie against a hot-water pipe that runs along the top of a tall cupboard in the kitchen. A slender, elegant cat, she walks with long, leisurely strides; then, preparing to jump, 'gathers' herself like a racehorse about to clear a fence. The next moment she is on the mantelpiece. Sitting up motionless, against the backcloth of a whitewashed wall, her coat a satin-smooth black and white, her eyes glinting emerald, she might be a rare porcelain ornament. Another leap and she is on the cupboard where, curling herself up, she peers from under the horizontal water-pipe, or in sleep, to quote Tessimond again, 'extends a velvet forepaw'.

Which is the more beautiful, feline movement or feline stillness? An impossible question.

Which is more beautiful, a bird poised on a branch or a bird on the wing?

One night in Paris, Madame Michelet was dining in a house facing the Café Turc where a ball was being held. On the roof opposite, above the ballroom, she counted nine cats moving sedately to the music, backs arched, paws rising and falling. Then all of a sudden, as the band finished playing the waltz and launched into a quadrille, they began to leap about as if out of their minds. Jellicle cats, T. S. Eliot assures us in *Old Possum's Book of Practical Cats*, can dance a jig and a gavotte; and Japanese legend tells of an annual cats' reunion which ends with a dance in the moonlight. To gain admittance, every cat has to bring a shawl or kerchief to wear on the head during the dance.

Richard Austin, an authority on ballet, has written the following on the subject of cats and the dance:

It is not surprising that choreographers have drawn on the movement of cats for their inspiration; the soft padding of a cat across the room is like a dance. Indeed to watch cats dart, leap, and run is to see a kind of ballet, since they have the same poise and elegance as dancers. One step in classical ballet, the *pas de chat*, suggests the dab of a paw; here, the dancer plays with the music as if it were a ball of wool.

The most famous cat-music in ballet is the *pas de deux* for Puss in Boots and the White Cat, by Tchaikovsky, in the last act of *The Sleeping Beauty*. Here the dancers parody the grand *pas de deux* of classical ballet, but at moments lose their poise to scratch at one another like a pair of angry kittens. The music recalls the wailing of two cats beneath the moon—a melancholy, amorous descant, swooningly out of tune.

Modern choreographers have also been inspired by cats— notably in Balanchine's *La Chatte*, set to music by Henri Sauget and created for perhaps the greatest of all classical ballerinas, Olga Spessivtzeva, who was incongruously dressed in talc and transparencies, much to her dislike; and in *Les Demoiselles de La Nuit*, composed by Roland Petit with a scenario by the French dramatist Jean Anouilh, whose leading role was created by Dame Margot Fonteyn, herself a lover of cats. In the role of Agathe, the white cat, Dame Margot was asked by the designer, Leonor Fini, to wear a cat mask complete with pink nose and whiskers, but refused, explaining in her autobiography that she could not conceive of expressing anything with her head 'shut in a kind of cat-box'.

The ballet had an ingenious set, giving a picture of the sloping roof-tops of Paris—the cats chasing one another over the tiles. Unfortunately the structure collapsed during the first night in Paris, leaving the dancers to bring the ballet to a close in a mass of splintered wood. No one was hurt, since dancers, like cats, rarely get injured when they fall.

A dancer can learn from a cat. A girl studying at the Royal Ballet

School told me that at home she could profitably watch for hours the movements of her cat Mirabelle: above all, the cat's poise in coming into a room; an ability, too, to 'freeze'—she was quoting Beverley Nichols—'into a posture of the utmost grace'. It was Beverley Nichols who said that part of a model's training should consist in watching a cat parading in front of her, and that no woman could manipulate her train with the grace with which a cat can twitch her tail.

In reflecting upon a creature whose movements are as agile, as varied, as graceful, as quick as are those of the cat, at what point, we may ask, do we draw a distinction between movement in a general sense and the dance? Look at a kitten chasing his tail. Look at Théophile Steinlen's drawings of a cat pursuing a ball of thread, or confronting the leaps and bounds of a frog. Even elderly cats can retain a remarkable grace and dignity of movement.

Musicians, too, have frequently been inspired by their cats. The music made by Domenico Scarlatti's cat as she padded up and down the harpsichord is said to have prompted him to compose the *Cat's Fugue*. Aaron Copland's *The Cat and the Mouse*, subtitled *Scherzo Humoriste*, evokes the leaping and bounding and scurrying of a mouser, and in Fauré's *Kitty Valse* we feel the lilt and frolic of a kitten at play. The reiterated miaows in Rossini's *Duetto Buffo di Due Gatti* (Cats' Duet) are sheer delight—especially as performed by Victoria de los Angeles and Elisabeth Schwarzkopf at Gerald Moore's farewell concert. Ravel's *L'Enfant et les Sortilèges* (The Child and the Spells)—the music his, the words Colette's—though mocked at first in Paris, has since been acclaimed as the composer's greatest work. As to Henri Sauget's *La Chatte*, when his cat Cody heard the *Petite Suite* he would roll on his back, shiver, jump on to the piano and lick his master's fingers. If the composer ceased to play, Cody would withdraw, then rush back when the music was resumed.

* * *

A treatise could be written on the language of the tail: so much can be deduced from the way it is held, the way in which it moves. But the personality of the particular cat must be borne in mind, since what applies to one cat need not apply to another.

Dr A. L. Rowse's Peter, when he was a newcomer, a diffident, 'gangling adolescent', held his tail awkwardly, to one side. As he grew in confidence and felt accepted, his tail changed into a splendid silvery white plume, held upright, swaying against the blue of hydrangeas and the blue of the Cornish sea.

The late Canon Liddon, who had a great affection for cats, including the common-room cat at Christ Church, Oxford, called the tail a 'catometer'. Thomas Gray, writing in his poem 'On the death of a favourite cat drowned in a tub of gold-fishes' of the 'pensive Selima', says that 'her conscious tail her joy declared'. And Calvin, the renowned cat belonging to the American writer Charles Dudley Warner, had, his master records, an 'expressive, slow-moving tail' which, if an unfamiliar cat appeared on the lawn, he expanded to a formidable size.

Aldous Huxley in *Sermons on Cats* calls the tail 'the principal organ of emotional expression', and goes on to compare tails to 'tapering serpents endowed, even when the cat lies in a sphinx-like repose, with a spasmodic uneasy life of their own'.

To lash the tail is usually taken as a sign of aggression, but this is not always so. Mysouff, the cat belonging to Alexandre Dumas, waved his tail in excitement when he saw his master approaching. Rudyard Kipling's 'cat that walked by himself', who roamed the wet wild woods and the wet wild roofs, lashed his tail not in anger but in triumphant satisfaction, because he had so settled his affairs that he had milk to drink and a hearth at which to sit, while at the same time remaining free to range at will. And the cat belonging to the son of a friend of mine, when left for a few days with this friend, lashes his tail against her legs until they ache, missing his master and his own home.

In Huxley's essay mentioned above a Siamese, neglected by her husband, pads around lashing her tail not through indignation but in a tragic gesture of despair. In contrast, her unfaithful spouse betrays his guilt by a droop of the tail. There are many reasons for a drooping tail. A cat can be preoccupied, or plain bored. Or take the little black cat in Harold Monro's poem, whose 'tail hangs loose' as she laps up her milk: clearly she is relaxed, at ease.

A gentle rhythmic movement of the tail, as distinct from a lashing or swishing, can denote quiet deliberation. To be or not to be? A twitching tail can indicate a similar mood—or sheer perversity.

A cat, for example, smells fish, demands some persistently. You prepare what you think is an attractive helping. The cat looks at it critically: sniffs, twitches his tail and saunters away as though in a huff. He is saying: 'Will I? ... Won't I? ... Perhaps ... Yes ... But in my own time.'

Twitching the tail can be a mannerism. A particular Russian Blue, having indicated that he wanted the door opened, would invariably give a double twitch to his tail as if, possibly, to stress the urgency of his request. The same cat used to come in through the window in the early morning: then, having jumped on to my bed and touched my cheek with his nose, would unfailingly twitch his tail before diving under the eiderdown.

A cat with tail held high is generally in good fettle. But don't jump to hasty conclusions. If the cat with whom you have been conversing stalks away, tail aloof, it may mean you have bored him stiff. If on the other hand the tail is held high but turned over at the tip, that is a sign of good humour.

* * *

Lastly, the language of facial expression. Ears, eyes, whiskers, all play a part. Pricked ears, pointing forward, indicate expectancy; ears turned back or lying flat denote displeasure, even anger. Look at the two cats in Jacopo Bassano's painting of the animals assembled to go into the Ark. Neither cat is pleased at being caught into this unruly throng: one is sulky, the other irritated by the proximity of a fussy cock and hen. Facial expression is again superbly conveyed in Jean Baptiste Chardin's eighteenth-century painting *La Raie*, which shows a cat, ears back, consumed with guilt, moving stealthily across a dining-table, one paw extended to seize at the auspicious moment a helping of fish.

The eyes of a cat can outstare a man, causing him no little discomfiture, or look through him as if he did not exist. A cat's eyes can assume, too, a strange expressionless pallor. When this is so, beware! If you have not yourself given offence, someone or something certainly has. Pupils suddenly dilating to an exceptional size can denote fear.

As to whiskers, you need to know the personality of the cat. A twitch can indicate disgust or disdain. On the other hand, I knew a cat who twitched his whiskers to show satisfaction, to say 'thank you'.

On the face of a cat you can read indifference, disgust, puzzlement, contentment, serenity. Take Renoir's *L'Enfant au Chat*: the cat's expression, the eyes half-closed, verges on ecstasy. In contrast, in Tsugoharu Foujita's *Girl with a Cat* the pale, silvery Persian has a restless, staring look in her eyes as if she would like to extricate herself from the arms that clasp her. Delacroix's *Head of a Cat*, whether it represents a domestic pet or a wild cat seen by the artist in Africa, has the look of calm nobility that characterises many members of the genus *Felis*. A particularly lively, if somewhat aggressive, cat is the cockney tabby in Hogarth's *The Graham Children*—in which, for sheer personality, the cat outshines the children. For an example of sinister cats, look at the two who, from the shadowy background of Goya's *Don Manuel Osorio de Zuñiga*, fix their gaze on the magpie held on a string by the little boy. And then there is the work of the illustrator Louis Wain. One cannot but admire his ability to convey on the faces of cats—inspired, I imagine, by his own cat Peter the Great—an expression of wide-eyed wonder or dismay, accentuated by a wrinkled brow.

One of the most expressive cats of all, not just in facial expression but in general alertness, is the little tortoiseshell in W. V. Mieris's seventeenth-century Dutch *Fish and Poultry Shop*, which can be seen in the National Gallery. The little cat misses nothing, and if you let him guide you you will miss nothing either.

9
Psychology and skills

As a rule people either like cats or dislike them. They are rarely indifferent.

Generally speaking, despots, as Rousseau reminded Boswell, dislike cats. (Cardinal Wolsey, Cardinal Richelieu and Mussolini were exceptions: Mussolini called the cat his favourite animal, admiring him for his intelligence and independence.) The point Rousseau made was that from the despot's angle the cat is unacceptable because he will not slavishly carry out orders: there can be no question of blind obedience on the part of a cat. When Boswell retorted that the same could be said of a hen, Rousseau replied that, whereas a hen would carry out orders if she could be made to understand what was required of her, the cat, even when he understands perfectly, still does not obey. That is, Rousseau explained, when a cat is under constraint: a cat who is genuinely attached to someone will do anything out of friendship.

Dislike of cats can range from distaste to mania. Boswell was ill at ease when in the same room as a cat, yet this did not prevent him from writing appreciatively of Dr Johnson's beloved Hodge. There are those, however, Shylock reminds us, who become mad if they so much as 'behold a cat'. Sir Walter Scott knew a man whose complexion, if he glimpsed a cat, assumed every colour that contributed to the plaid of his kilt. Napoleon did not need to see the animal: he sensed its presence. One night in the palace of Schönbrunn in Vienna he was found in his room, sweat pouring down his face, a sword in his hand, lunging frantically and ineffectually at a tapestry behind which, it transpired, a cat was asleep, unaware of the furore.

In a study in the *Nursing Times* of treatment given to a victim suffering from cat phobia, the writers, a psychologist and a nurse, emphasise the young woman's fear of the animal's eyes: a symptom, in her instance, associated with childhood memories of the terror experienced by not only herself but by her mother and her grandmother when confronted with a cat's eyes glowing in the darkness. The girl dreamed, she says, of black cats with green eyes. She was unnerved, too, by pictures of cats in magazines: 'I couldn't escape the look in their eyes.'

Her doctors required her to look repeatedly at such photographs, even though she felt that the cats 'looked right through' her. The treatment, supported by her own efforts of will and by the friendliness and playfulness of a large cat called Smokey whose services were called upon, proved therapeutic. She can now say: 'I enjoy cats and could listen to stories about them all day.'

The therapeutic qualities of the cat are not sufficiently recognised. A cat can bring comfort to the sick, the bereaved, the lonely, the depressed, the old.

Some years ago a Dr Rudd, at the geriatric hospital in Lymington, Hampshire, introduced, to alleviate the loneliness of the patients, a couple of resident cats for each ward. They went on duty at specified times, wandering from bed to bed, making a great fuss of the patients, snuggling into their arms. An interesting point is that whereas cats have a reputation for making their presence felt just where they are not wanted, these kept away from patients who disliked cats, as if knowing intuitively the purpose of their visits.

Needless to say, some people disapproved of their presence in the wards. The matron, however, stoutly supported the doctor's experiment. Cats, she said, are clean, gentle, and quiet—admirably suited to the elderly.

Some people have difficulty in coming to terms with the cat's detachment, his tendency to return affection only when it suits him. Chateaubriand was attracted by this feline wilfulness, self-possession, aloofness—this ability to pass unperturbed 'from the salon to the roof tops'. The poet W. H. Davies found cats 'strange' and 'frightening', yet loved his own 'black Venus of a cat'. A typical representative of this ambivalent attitude is Hilaire Belloc. In his essay 'On Them' (to him cats are a mysterious 'they' or 'them') he dwells on his disike and fear, and yet he was known to travel accompanied by his cat in a basket.

Besides, with what charming irony, with what perceptivity, does he write, in 'A Conversation with a Cat', of the tawny, elegant, majestic Amalthea bestowing upon him, uninvited, her tenderness, her 'purring beatitude'! In a dreary station bar, where the tube trains come to their terminus in district 'S.W.99', she brings solace to his loneliness, comfort to his melancholy. Yes, he decides, in

Amalthea he has found a friend who will never leave him, whose company he will share, the two sitting together 'through all un-counted time'.

But no. The dream fades. As lovely as a wave, Amalthea leaps lightly to the floor, strolls away without a backward look. Then the final insult: she coolly, graciously, responds to the advances of a layabout hanging around for a drink.

* * *

The novelist George Moore used to tell his friends how in Dublin, after the Irish Rebellion, while meandering in the region of Henry Street, he came upon the ruined wall of a house to which there clung the wreckage of a mantelpiece. Hearing a plaintive mew, he saw a splendid black Persian close to the fireplace. The cat was clearly pleased to see him, yet could not be enticed from the once familiar hearth. Marvelling at the beauty of the cat and his fidelity, Moore continued to search among the debris, where he found numerous cats looking for their now devastated homes, unable to grasp what had happened. 'Cats suffer vaguely,' Moore commented. 'But suffering', he would go on, 'is not less painful because it is vague.'

There are people who say glibly that cats care only for places, not for persons. Certainly cats care for places. But this does not mean that they are indifferent to persons. George Moore shows, I think, how close in certain respects cats are to ourselves. For many are the human beings who, consciously or unconsciously, carry through the years, perhaps through life, a nostalgia for a lost home, a paradise from which they feel themselves barred. And when we look back, we recall not only a house and its surroundings (however lovely these may have been), but the persons who made these into what they became: a home, and all this word implies. That is what the cats in Henry Street were looking for: the familiar chair, the favourite window-sill, the glowing hearth; the hand held out to caress. We humans can to some extent analyse our plight. The cats can only suffer 'vaguely', as a bewildered child suffers, who, in a crowd, has lost hold of a parent's hand.

The cat instinctively seeks the familiar. A correspondent in a Sunday paper remarked how her cat chose always to sit on the eighth step of a flight of stairs—not the seventh or ninth, always the eighth. This brought another letter telling of the return home, after an absence of eight years, of a family accompanied by their big tabby cat. When at the door of the house the cat was let out of his basket, he went straight to the nearby railway embankment and sprang on to the very same fence-post which had been his favourite spot all those years ago.

In *The Story of my Cats*, the nineteenth-century naturalist Henri Fabre tells of the impact made upon a dynasty of ginger cats by a move from Avignon, first to Orange, then to Sérignan. The females, released from their baskets, inspected their new abode, gave little surprised miaows and questioning glances. Within a day or so, however, caresses and saucers of milk had allayed apprehensions. Not so in the case of the toms. One of the three, in his zeal to reach his old home, braved the swirling water of the river Sorgue. A second, frightened and bewildered by his unfamiliar surroundings, was found lying dead in the ashes by the hearth. He had died of grief, Fabre says—and Fabre was no sentimentalist. The third tom, having swum across a torrential river, reached his former home, his coat caked with red mud. After that he disappeared. He was last seen hiding behind a hedge, a rabbit in his mouth: he had 'gone wild'. Fabre makes the point that the cats in question did not cross the river by one of several bridges, which would have been easier but longer: a cat, he explains, instinctively travels, if possible, 'as the crow flies'.

* * *

St George Mivart, the English biologist and authority on Felidae, whose masterful study *The Cat* (1881) remains important to our understanding of all aspects of this fascinating family of animals, makes the point that only by becoming cats could we completely understand their minds. This explains the generally unsatisfactory nature of cat stories told in the first person, and of pictures of cats wearing human clothes—though there are exceptions, among them the illustrations of Gérard Grandville and Louis Wain. I have a soft spot, too, for the semi-human cat Behemoth in Mikhail Bulgakov's novel *Master and Margarita*, who plays chess, smears oysters with mustard, catches a slither of playing-cards in mid-air, stands in a queue, fare in paw, waiting to board a tram.

Mivart's remark does not mean, of course, that we cannot with observation and patience learn a great deal about cat psychology. And if we have anything to do with cats this is necessary, for their sakes and our own.

A cat commands respect. It is an insult, as I have already suggested, to talk to him in cloying, infantile language. If you take the trouble to watch the face of a cat addressed in this manner you need not be surprised to see an expression of not mere bewilderment but distaste, even disdain. Colette knew what she was doing when she made a point of speaking to her cat reasonably and clearly. This is not to say that a cat does not like terms of endearment. He does. But these should be well chosen and worthy of a creature who values self-respect. A woman who has made a considerable study of cats notices how many of them, no matter what their nationality, appreciate being spoken to in musical tongues—Italian and other romance languages.

We in Britain can learn from attitudes elsewhere. A friend of mine who worked at an American base at Keflavik, Iceland, wrote:

Most Icelanders, in particular veterinary surgeons, deplore any kind of sentimentality which robs animals of their dignity. It is looked upon as a serious offence to tie ribbons on pets, feed them on the wrong diet, address them in 'baby-talk' ... Dogs and cats need space to roam; it is, therefore, considered cruel to keep them in confined spaces for selfish human enjoyment. Anyone found keeping a cat in a flat for an indefinite period is fined—at least in the city of Reykjavik.

And Ernest Renan, the French writer and historian, learned an unforgettable lesson from his training with the Jesuits: *la politesse même vers les animaux* (courtesy even to animals). He was never known to turn a cat out of a chair.

It is important that affection be shown. Independent though the cat is, he craves affection. Consider the ways in which he responds: an arching of the back, a sweeping caress with the tail, kneading with the claws, a thrust of the head against the hand, a purr. But he does not like to be clutched, squeezed, mauled, 'slobbered over'. Children should be taught these elementary facts while they are young, so that cat and child can enjoy each other's companionship without detriment to either. Try any nonsense in handling a cat and he will quickly extricate himself—probably with dignity; but, if provoked, he is not averse to putting out his claws. And who can blame him?

Remember, too, that much as a cat appreciates affection, he will not ask for it unless he trusts the person completely, knows from long experience that the affection is there awaiting him. If he has been ignored, rebuffed, or treated casually he will keep his distance: he is too proud to do otherwise.

Affection fosters confidence. A cat, if he has not learnt confidence and self-reliance in kittenhood, can grow up insecure, timorous, unresponsive. Feline psychology and child psychology have much in common. Like a child, a kitten needs attention. Kittens who are picked up frequently, yet carefully and gently, normally open their eyes earlier than others, are more sociable, more exploratory, more enterprising, more resilient. A kitten should have toys to play with —a ball, some old wool, a furry animal and so on. The more 'experiences' the better, provided common sense is observed. A kitten who never sets eyes on a child may grow up shy of children. Indeed, in the case of a cat, the 'finished product'—if one may put it so—reflects the owner. If the owner is distant, dull, unsociable, the cat is likely to develop similar traits. It is, however, only right to concede that the fault does not always lie with human beings. There are cats who are dim-witted—plain dull. No effort on our part will make them otherwise; but cats of this kind are a minority.

A cat can be as emotionally disturbed as a human. Jealousy can be the cause. If a new cat is introduced into a home in which one is already established, this must be done with circumspection. An older cat must not be allowed to feel left out, or that affection has been deflected from him. Grief can, literally, be discerned on the face of an elderly cat who by the arrival of a skittish newcomer is made to feel *de trop*. This need not happen. If the new cat is brought in unobtrusively, if the first is made much of, his seniority acknowledged and emphasised, he will often take the other under his wing, initiate him into the ways of the household and, given time, become fond of him.

A cat can be jealous of a child. A student friend of mine, Susanna Edney, and her husband Kenneth found a tiny orange kitten, ill and abandoned, among some dustbins. Thanks to their care he grew into a splendid cat, highly intelligent and devoted to them both. They called him Mango. All was well until their first baby was born, when Mango became inordinately jealous. He did not attempt to hurt the child; he showed his hostility by attacking her belongings. Finally he stole the blanket from her cot, dragged it down the garden and tried to hide it. The baby, when she reached the stage of being able to crawl, retaliated by making her way into the kitchen and eating Mango's dinner, which was on a dish under the table!

A cat can be the friend of a creature of a completely different species. Gilbert White, in *The Natural History of Selborne*, tells how an acquaintance of his, sitting one evening in the garden, saw his cat trotting towards him, calling—'with little short inward notes of complacency'—to a leveret gambolling behind. The cat had reared this leveret, supporting it 'with great affection'.

When Richard Steele (1672–1729), Irish man of letters, reached home in the evening he would pet his cat, poke the fire, then sit down between cat and dog. The two animals got on well for, having been brought up together, they had acquired certain of each other's habits. 'The Dog', Steele wrote in the *Tatler*, 'gives himself the airs of a Cat and the Cat . . . affects the behaviour of the little Dog.'

There is also Mark Twain's story of a cat in the zoo at Marseilles, who used to clamber up an elephant's hind leg, then spend half the afternoon on the animal's back, dozing in the sunshine. At first the elephant was annoyed and would use his trunk to lift the cat down. In vain: the cat went 'aft' and clambered up again. After a while the two were close friends.

Photographs by Rod Brindamour, reproduced in the *National Geographical Magazine* of October 1975, show a three-year-old orang-utan playing with his friend, a tabby. The cat puts up with most things, asserting her freedom only when her companion stretches her out, full length, as though on the rack. Compliance is all very well, but enough is enough—and out come the claws.

There are many recorded instances of friendship between racehorses and cats. George Stubbs, in his painting of the Arab stallion Godolphin, who died in 1753, includes a black cat. Arthur Thompson of Arlington Park Race Track, California, remarks on the 'special affinity between horse and cat'. There each stable has its pet, be it no more than a hen; but the most popular are cats, who like to sleep under the manger or on the horse's back. In the mid-thirties Fet, the horse who won the Cesarewitch three times, had as stable companions a goat and a black tom, and would not be bedded down unless these two were with him; and P. G. Wodehouse's story *Catnappers* turns on the attempt, frustrated by Bertie Wooster and Jeeves, to kidnap the feline friend of the favourite in the hope that the horse would be too despondent to do himself justice.

* * *

Catus amat piscem sed non vult tangere plantas: 'the cat likes fish, but doesn't like to get his paws wet', runs an old saying.

Gilbert White, remarking on the 'violent fondness of cats for fish', notes that of all quadrupeds they are the least disposed to wet a paw, much less enter water. Writing in the latter half of the eighteenth century, he would not have known about Turkish Vann

'Turkish Vann cats . . . enjoy both swimming and frolicking in water.'

cats—chalk-white, fluffy cats with amber markings, bushy amber tails, and large paws—who enjoy both swimming and frolicking in water. A girl I know stayed with a family in Las Palmas who had brought one of these cats with them from Turkey. (Do not ask how they evaded the health authorities!) The little cat, in high spirits, accompanied the children whenever they went swimming.

Charlie, a blond Burmese with a touch of ginger, nipped one day at low tide across the Thames from Chiswick Mall to Chiswick Eyot to catch rats. When he wanted to come home the tide was in. Undaunted, he swam. After that, people living on houseboats became used to the 'swimming cat'. One day of exceptional flooding, the river police had to bring him back. Now nearly ten years old, he swims less, but there is no knowing what else he will be up to. He sneaks into the back of parked cars, lies low, then, later, leaps on to the shoulder of an unsuspecting driver. He has been returned by enraged motorists from various places in the Home Counties. There was also the Sunday when, after disappearing along the towpath, he was brought home by a nun. He had turned up in church, where he caused consternation by miaowing throughout the hymn-singing!

The late Carl van Vechten, author of *Tiger in the House* (1921), had an orange Persian called Ariel who enjoyed taking a bath: he would jump eagerly into the water.

A country cat, I am told, used to take herself on hot days to a spot where an overflow pipe ran out of a well. Here she would lie down in about three inches of water, submerging first one side, then the other, after which, soaking wet except for her head, she would make for home. There she lay on the carpet in front of the empty fireplace and licked herself until she was dry.

C. H. Ross, in *The Book of Cats* (1868), writes of a cat called Puddles who used to dive into the water at Newcastle-on-Tyne to catch minnows, pilchards and eels. In *Rabbits, Cats and Cavies* (1903) C. H. Lane goes one better when he tells of a fisherman's cat who, having learnt as a kitten to swim, liked to accompany his owner to sea. If left behind, he sat on the beach howling horribly. His favourite place was in the bow, from where he watched the dogfish: 'When they were thick all about, he would dive in and fetch 'em out, jammed in his mouth as fast as may be, just as if they were a parcel of rats.'

On the ship on which Chateaubriand crossed the Atlantic when he was twenty-three was a tabby with 'bushy whiskers' who had sailed twice around the world. Experience had taught him how to 'stand firm on his paws' so that, however much the vessel pitched and tossed, he kept his balance. A favourite with the crew, he was privileged to sleep on the second mate's fur coat.

Mark Twain, writing of the *Oceanea*, a large, stately ship, mentions three big friendly cats who walked all over the ship, a white one following the steward. One of them, when the ship put in—whether in England, Australia, or India—used to go ashore and not be seen again until the day of sailing. How did he know the date and time? The crew conjectured that he came down to the dock each day, and, when he saw passengers and baggage going aboard, concluded that he had better do the same.

* * *

Christopher Smart, in the mysterious and obscure poem about his cat Jeoffry, 'Jubilate Agno', says that the cat

> made a great figure in Egypt for his signal services.
> For he killed the Icneumon-rat very pernicious by land.

Apart from killing rodents, it was long believed that the cat was able to cure the bite of a serpent, snake or asp. After all, was it not Ra the Great Cat who slew Apep the serpent of evil? And there is the story about the snake who slithered up Muhammad's arm, inside the sleeve of his robe. Asked by the prophet to depart, it refused. 'Well, then,' said Muhammad, 'let us refer the matter to the cat.' And so the cat asked the snake to put out its head, that they might discuss the matter more easily. The snake did so, whereupon the cat pounced and killed it.

Down the years the cat has remained the triumphant opponent of the snake. Whereas other creatures shrink from encountering one, the cat will normally lift his paw unperturbed and with a single, well-aimed blow slay his enemy.

When a promontory of Cyprus was infested with black-and-white snakes, cats from a neighbouring monastery were dispatched to exterminate them. This they did at set hours, methodically and efficiently. At mealtimes the monastery bell rang and the cats returned for refreshment and relaxation. The promontory came to be known as the Cape of the Cats.

In Paraguay cats hunting rattlesnakes have been known to struggle with their opponents for hours on end, always emerging victorious.

In June 1971 a Mrs Winstone and her husband, a civil engineer, were living in Sumatra. The household included Widger, a cat belonging to their cook: a large snow-white animal with a black tail who walked about the bungalow as if he were king of the castle. 'There were times', Mrs Winstone says, 'when we were a little frightened of Widger. Not that he was aggressive. Quite the opposite. It was his majestic regal air: it made us fear we might in some way offend him.'

One sultry afternoon Mr and Mrs Winstone were dozing on the verandah when they were wakened with a start by Widger. Looking down they saw a green, venomous snake a few feet away. 'My first inclination', Mrs Winstone recalls, 'was to spring up from my chair, had it not been for my husband's restraining arm and a whispered warning not to frighten the snake into action.' It was Widger who knew what to do. Back arched and snarling like a dog, he proceeded to bounce up and down to attract the snake's attention. Little by little the snake reared; then, lowering its head, moved towards the cat. Widger backed slowly, still snarling and spitting as the snake slithered towards him.

From the verandah, husband and wife watched the final action. The snake was three or four feet away from the white bouncing cat when it struck out. Widger avoided the attack by springing into the air, and, making a circle, landed on the verandah. Mrs Winstone went to pick up the cat, who had flopped down exhausted, while the snake retreated into the undergrowth.

Widger was never quite the same again. It turned out that he had a heart condition. Some months later, when Mr and Mrs Winstone were back in England, they heard that the cat had died. In his memory they planted a rose bush in the garden.

* * *

Apart from their less obvious services to man—Mallarmé claimed that a cat was useful in the home because she kept the furniture polished—numerous cats are and have been public employees, paid to keep rodents at bay in post offices, government offices, factories, docks, institutions and even the Houses of Parliament.

In December 1976 there was a sensation in Manchester, when dockers protested at management's decision to cut the allowances granted to provide rations for the cat Mandy, mouser-in-chief, and her assistants: the cats, it was argued, were no longer killing rodents on the same scale as previously. The charge gave rise to indignation. Mr Philip Joyce, protesting on behalf of the Boiler-makers' Union, said that the cats, far from being idle, bore in many instances the scarred faces and torn ears of true fighters.

Another mouser of distinction was Blacky, employed at the GPO headquarters at St Martin-le-Grand. Jason, a gentle white cat with dark markings, besides being mouser at St Paul's Cathedral, also kept a watchful eye on the sandwiches of the stonemasons, whose work plainly intrigued him—as did their transistor radio, to which he listened intently, preferring classical music. At Bedford Park, Essex, the official ratcatcher, a great tabby called Peanuts, lost an eye—but not his courage or zeal—while carrying out his duties. In 1973 Wilberforce, white with black splotches and a black tail, was requisitioned from the RSPCA to deal with vermin at Downing Street: the police were instructed to ring the front door-bell at any hour, day or night, to let him in. Tiger, 'the Terror of the Ritz', a colossal mouser fed on every luxury, has to be sent away annually on a slimming course.

Since 1883 the Home Office has had a succession of mousers, mostly males and all, regardless of sex, named Peter. In 1964 a Manx cat was presented by the Lieutenant-General of the Isle of Man.

In the British Museum in the early years of this century lived Black Jack, friend of the late Dr Richard Garnett, Keeper of the Department of Printed Books, who composed the well-known lines about his own cat Marigold:

> Her back was arched, her tail was high.
> A green fire glared in her vivid eye;
> And all the Toms, though never so bold,
> Quailed at the martial Marigold.

Black Jack's favourite place was the Reading Room, where he would sit by the hour on a table, regardless of the inconvenience he might cause. When he wanted to go out, he expected the folding doors to be held open. One day, having been accidentally shut in, he whiled away the time by sharpening his claws on the bindings that enclosed newspapers. As a penalty he was banned by officialdom, then reported as 'missing, presumed dead'. However, to the joy of all reasonable persons he reappeared, and from then on was respectfully referred to as the Reading Room Cat.

Black Jack was succeeded by Mike, a cockney tabby—something of a rapscallion. While still a kitten he was brought in one day by Black Jack and laid at the feet of the Keeper of Egyptian Mummies, who became his friend. Mike also made friends with the gatekeeper, who allotted to him a comfortable place in the lodge and, during the lean years of World War I, saw that he was well fed. Mike was pernickety about food: he preferred sole to whiting, whiting to haddock—for cod he had no use at all. He died on 15 January 1929, aged twenty, deeply mourned.

* * *

Cats have long played a role in advertising. A window-bill of about 1884, now in the Bodleian Library, Oxford, shows a snarling bulldog held at bay by a length of J & P Coats sewing-machine cotton. A couple of cats—a tabby and a black—watch, with expressions of mingled surprise and satisfaction, the dog's ineffectual efforts to free himself. A third cat, another tabby, looks on complacently, his forepaws, crossed one over the other, resting on a cotton reel.

As lovers of warmth, cats in various guises appear from roughly 1860 onwards on matchboxes. A revival of interest in cats at this period probably emanated from Queen Victoria, who had a cat called White Heather but was specially fond of tabbies. Hence the numerous paintings of large sleepy tabbies reclining on tasselled cushions, and also the popularity of cats on Christmas cards.

Few people will have forgotten the late Arthur, the big white television cat who died on 1 March 1976. Had he lived another month he would have been seventeen. A personality, promoter of some million tins of cat food, loved by thousands, protected by

'Arthur ... featured in television advertisements for eighteen weeks each year and starred in thirty-five films.'

security guards, he lived a colourful, eventful life. Press conferences were held for him; his biography was read during his lifetime. He was twice kidnapped and for three days was involved in a High Court case to decide who, legally, was his owner. The judge, to whom Arthur was solemnly introduced in court, after addressing him with the greatest courtesy, gave custody to Spillers.

If Arthur had been a member of Equity he would have made an immense fortune. He featured in television advertisements for eighteen weeks each year and starred in thirty-five films. His habit of extracting food from the tin with his left paw endeared him to onlookers. After his death one of his admirers, a nine-year-old girl, gave up watching television. 'I can't bear TV without Arthur', she sobbed. 'He was such a *comfortable* cat!'

Familiar from hoardings, buses and magazines is a splendid silvery Persian with dark, thoughtful eyes: Lewishof, Michael of Jemari, winner of prizes in the United States and England and prime salesman of Kossett carpets. Another cat sells refrigerators.

Black (or, to be exact, prune-coloured), as stately as a bronze cat of ancient Egypt, sleek and elegant, she sits bolt upright, wears a high, close-fitting diamonté collar worthy of a dowager.

In the advertising world of the United States the equivalent of Arthur has been Morris, the 'finicky cat', the 'super cat', the 'star' who eats only the particular food which he condescends to publicise. A big burly marmalade-coloured animal with thick short fur who began life as a stray, he now appears on television, on hoardings, in journals and in magazines. Sometimes he is accompanied by a greyish kitten who is obviously, in Morris's opinion, a little flibberti-gibbet totally lacking in gastronomical discernment, ready to gobble up anything—a cat with no class, no style.

In the fall of 1972 a contest was organised to find a cat who would match in appearance, intelligence and charm this heart-throb of many a human. Boston, Buffalo, Baltimore, Cleveland, Pittsburgh were just a few of the cities visited by Morris in person, and at each place photograph after photograph of feline competitors poured in. Cats of every colour and breed were entered. One snapshot of a small black cat was accompanied by a letter to the effect that, although on the outside this puss bore little resemblance to Morris, inside he *was* Morris!

Finally, there was a whirlwind weekend during which Morris entertained Gillie, the winner of the competition, in Chicago, his home town. The programme included, for the two cats, a drive through the city in a limousine, a lunch of tuna fish served with white wine at Maxime de Paris, one of Chicago's most opulent restaurants, and a visit to an aquarium exhibiting rare breeds of fish which swam to and fro within inches of the cats' faces. The photographs of Morris and his guest are revealing—Morris some-what blasé, Gillie a little bewildered!

* * *

A theatre needs a cat—not, as a rule, as a performer, but rather to supervise, see that things are up to the mark, keep rodents at bay, inspect corridors, tunnels, stairways, know his way among screens and curtains, in and out of unfamiliar doors, up and down ill-lit steps. This kind of thing cats take in their stride.

Theatre cats vary considerably. T. S. Eliot's 'Gus' (an abbreviation of Asparagus), the cat at the theatre door, is elderly and 'as thin as a rake', but a 'character' not to be trifled with.

Bouncer, the imposing silver tabby at the Garrick, is much admired, and can inspire awe. Sometimes he encounters a visiting Shih Tzu. Then sparks fly. Bouncer, however, is beyond doubt the boss.

At the Adelphi, Plug, a sleek, serious-minded black cat with white paws and a dab of white here and there on his coat, patrols the stalls with his sister, Socket. Both attend rehearsals, but discreetly absent themselves from shows.

Ambrose of Drury Lane saunters around with a somewhat superior air, looking from a distance as if he were in evening dress —black jacket and immaculate shirtfront. During *A Chorus Line* he coolly walked across the stage and was greeted with a round of applause.

When the Covent Garden market moved out of its old home there was an influx of rats in the neighbouring buildings. They took over the Aldwych Theatre. Eventually four cats were brought in, who during a single night disposed of the vermin. The present cat-in-charge is a black half-Persian with brilliant green eyes. At 6.30 each evening he is on duty in the foyer, welcoming members of the audience. He receives as big a fan-mail as many an actor.

Respected, revered, loved, regarded as a harbinger of good luck, a theatre cat can nevertheless be a source of embarrassment. In New York, during Henry Irving's first performance of *Faust*, a cat elected to stalk across the stage in the middle of the thunderstorm, then coolly took up his position on an imitation boulder from which he viewed the action. The attention of the audience was momentarily diverted and there was some tittering. Irving, however, was unperturbed; he took it as a good omen.

It was quite another matter—indeed the last straw—when a cat 'walked on' in the course of a disastrous performance of *The Barber of Seville*. Within seconds the already restless audience was transformed into a howling, jeering mob.

Any attempt to train a cat to 'perform' is a waste of time unless he himself chooses to co-operate. It is not that the cat lacks skill. He can do all sorts of things if he chooses: jump through a hoop, balance on a rubber ball, walk a tightrope, and so on. But will he?

A visitor to Paris, after watching a troupe of animals perform at the Folies Bergère, told a friend about a cat who did all manner of 'turns'. The friend was incredulous. He had been to a previous performance when the same cat, apart from cuffing a monkey, did nothing. When the trainer tried to coax her, she had darted up a ladder and for the entire evening sat on the top rung watching what was going on below.

The secret, probably, is to invite and encourage . . . and leave it at that. A few years ago Gerald Freedman, the producer of the Broadway hit *Colette*, felt that an essential facet of the heroine was lacking, namely her devotion to cats. To rectify this he introduced two cats into the performance, a ginger called Jason and Achille, a black-and-white. There was no question of their being constrained to play a role. They were simply given the freedom of the theatre. When brought in for the first couple of rehearsals they were unduly excited, dashing all over the place, but after a few days they settled down. To help them feel at home they were fed on the stage and allowed to roam at will. Jason was friendly and playful from the first. Achille was inclined to be aloof until the day of the dress rehearsal, when a red chair appeared on the stage which he immediately appropriated.

Viewed at first with suspicion and veiled disapproval by the actors, the cats soon became the darlings of the cast, and were fed on shrimps, chicken and other dainties. Having settled down, they romped around and frolicked at will. On the other hand, they showed an extraordinary sense of what was fitting—padding quietly across the stage, observing silence, and sitting motionless at appropriate moments.

The performance of Jason was highly satisfactory, but Achille had an extraordinary sense of what was required of him. 'You'd think he'd been to a drama school,' someone remarked. His sense of timing was impeccable. He possessed, his producer said, 'that ineffable quality called talent'. There was no question of coaxing the cats, no exercising of pressure. A taste of catnip before a performance was an asset, but not essential.

The truth, as Ian Niall wrote in *Country Life*, is that no one can train cats: they are 'two jumps ahead'. 'Anyone who thinks he is a cat trainer is a bit of a Münchhausen . . . No one tames cats. Cats tame people.'

10

Mysteries of the cat

Mon chat est un compagne mystique. The words were written by Mallarmé about his cat Neige, with whom he was happy to spend whole days alone. But the adjective *mystique*, suggestive of the visionary, is frequently applicable, whether one has in mind a cat created by an artist or writer or a particular living cat. Time and again there is, in a cat, an element that defies words, something to be felt rather than defined.

I can meditate repeatedly on Edouard Manet's lithograph *Rendezvous des Chats*, which shows, against a backcloth of rooftops, chimney-pots and moonlit, cloud-shredded sky, a Machiaevellian black tom (look at the crafty eye!) courting a scarcely less artful, ghost-pale queen.

The association between moon and cat reaches into a remote past. Some legends say that the moon created the cat, others that the moon is a giant cat who chases mice—shreds of cloud—across the sky. According to a Hindu saying, a cat seeing moonbeams reflected in a bowl of water will lap them, supposing them to be milk.

Vulson de la Colombière, the seventeenth-century authority on heraldry, was one of those who believed in the influence exercised on the cat by the moon. On the darkest night, he says, the cat's clear-sighted shining eyes change in size to match the moon. For as the moon, according as it participates in the light of the sun, changes its face from day to day, in like manner is the cat affected by the moon, the pupils of his eyes increasing and decreasing according as the heavenly body waxes or wanes.

Think, too, of the elderly cat of whom Ted Hughes writes in 'Esther's Tomcat'. He lies asleep through the day like 'a bundle of old rope'; then, when night falls, opens his eyes 'green as ring-stones' and

Walks upon sleep, his mind on the moon.

Or think of W. B. Yeats, the poet, who came of a cat-loving family. Think of his jet-black spell-bound cat Minnaloushe, creeping through the grass, running through the grass, 'alone, important and wise', lifting

> to the changing moon
> His changing eyes.

The eyes of the cat are large in proportion to the size of the head, and beautiful in their variety. Even the Comte de Buffon, who disliked cats, conceded that in dusk and darkness their eyes glittered like diamonds. Moreover blue eyes, such as those of Siamese, are prone, when the light is dim, to assume a ruby glow, as Neville Braybrooke notes in his poem 'Reflection in a cat's eyes'.

The unique quality of the cat's eye is emphasised by Mivart in a letter he quotes, written by a friend who, at his request, has examined a cat's eyes by means of an ophthalmoscope:

> I owe you thanks for directing my attention to one of the most beautiful things I have ever seen. Imagine a dense, yet luminous velvety-blackness below, bounded by a nearly horizontal line, just above which is a pearly spot: the entrance of the optic nerve. This presents the usual vessels emerging from it. The disc is surrounded by a sapphire blue zone of intense brilliancy, passing into metallic green; and beyond this the *tapetum* [the roundish patch which gives the eyes of cats their luminous appearance] shines out with glorious colours of pink and gold, with a shimmer of blue and green. It is really lovely.

According to an Irish legend, a cat's eyes are windows enabling us to see into another world.

Similarly, Pierre Loti writes of his cat Moumouthe Chinoise:

> No sooner has he realised I am alone than he comes and sits in front of me, assuming suddenly an expression seen now and again on the faces of those enigmatic, pensive creatures who belong to the same genus as he does. His yellow eyes gaze up at me, wide open, the pupils dilated in an effort of mind to question and to

'A cat's eyes are windows enabling us to see into another world.'

understand. 'Who are you, I wonder?' he asks. 'Why do I trust you?' 'What is your purpose in the world?'

Compare with this a passage in *Ich und Du* (I and Thou, 1937) in which the Hebrew philosopher Martin Buber reflects upon the mystery in the gaze of animals—the gaze of eyes that speak a language. Looking into the eyes of his cat he recognises, as they light up in response to his glance, a quality of amazement, of enquiry as though asking: 'What concern am I to you?' Or 'What existence have I in your sight?' Or 'What is it you would communicate to me?'

There is a gulf. Therein, a mystery. And yet, though it be only for a moment, this gulf is bridged.

* * *

It is difficult to convey in English that awareness, so striking in cats though not confined to them, of things of which most humans are quite unconscious. We can talk about a sixth sense, the occult, paraphysical phenomena, precognition and so forth. I prefer the words of Ronsard: *Le chat a l'esprit prophétique.* The phrase combines mystery with a lightness of touch. It is not dogmatic; it leaves you free to think as you choose. If the incident carries conviction, well and good; if not, you can dismiss it from your mind. Not everyone will believe the Chinese tradition that a cat, if he gives his mind to it, can cause the dead to rise.

A. L. Rowse tells how in his home in Cornwall his white cat, Peter, unnerved him for two or three nights on end by following with his eyes something invisible to Dr Rowse that moved around the room along the cornice of the ceiling.

I recall, in Somerset during World War II, a pair of tabbies who, each time enemy planes passed overhead on their way to bomb Bristol, used to yowl in a most sinister manner before the approaching planes became audible to human ears. It is true, of course, that cats' hearing is sharper than our own; but if this is the sole explanation, why did the pair yowl only at the approach of enemy aircraft, and not when Allied planes were overhead?

Again in World War II an elderly woman, when there was not time to reach the air-raid shelter, used to seek protection, with her cat, dog and canary, under an oak dining-table. One day she was standing in the porch when, without warning, her cat, who was in the garden, gave a sudden leap and dashed indoors under the table. She followed, taking with her the dog and the canary. A few minutes later a bomb exploded in the garden, demolished the porch and blew in the windows. Had it not been for the cat, they would have been killed, all four of them.

A family evacuated from the south-east to Exeter told me of their astonishment one evening at seeing swarms of cats walking calmly and purposefully along the road leading out into the country in the direction of Tiverton. That night came a devastating raid on Exeter. This incident was confirmed in the press in 1977 by a correspondent now living in Harrogate.

C. H. Lane, in his book *Rabbits, Cats and Cavies,* tells the weird story of two cats who were pets on board the destroyer HMS *Salmon.* On the morning preceding this ship's final disastrous voyage these cats, who had never before shown the slightest inclination to be gone. All other attempts having failed, just as the *Salmon* was weighing anchor the pair of them took a leap on to HMS *Sturgeon* which was lying alongside, thus saving their lives.

Richard Austin tells an eerie story of a different quality. One evening, in the kitchen of a country house in Ireland, the butler in a rage threw a potato at the cat, hitting him in the face. The cat retaliated with a yowl—no ordinary yowl, but prolonged, chilling the blood. The other servants shuddered. They were unanimous in affirming that they had heard not just the yowl, but actual words, addressed to the butler: 'I was here before you came,' the cat said. 'And I'll still be here when you've gone.' Next morning the butler dropped dead.

*   *   *

There are numerous accounts of phantom cats. Chateaubriand, in his *Mémoires d'outre-tombe*, tells of the ghost of the Comte de Combourg which appears from time to time on the staircase of the château. On occasions only the count's wooden leg appears, moving step by step, accompanied by an imposing black cat.

Other stories, though on the surface less dramatic, become perhaps even more so when set in the context of ordinary daily life . . .

Alison was a down-to-earth Scot. In twenty-five years she had not fully adjusted herself to Swedish life: she felt lonely. Then at Malmö a kindly family, sensing this, asked her to live with them, and knowing her affection for cats gave her a ginger-and-white kitten called Per.

On summer evenings Per, wearing harness and lead, accompanied her on walks in the forest. When Alison sat on a tree-stump reading, Per would sit contentedly beside her. There were excursions, too, into the country, Per sitting up on the lap of Sven, the little son of Alison's hostess, looking out of the window of the car.

When Per was five, Alison won a prize in the form of a holiday in Finland. To take the cat was impossible, but she knew the family would look after him. However, his obvious distress as her departure drew near caused her misgivings. For the first time, he growled and spat at her, scratched at her suitcases, chewed the straps of her rucksack, would not touch his meals. On the morning she left for Helsinki, Per had to be shut away, so aggressive had he become.

Never had Alison enjoyed such a gay, exciting holiday. The first week sped by. For the eighth day an outing to the north of Finland had been planned.

During the previous night, however, Alison suddenly awoke from a vague, frightening dream. She had heard, she was convinced, the mewing of a cat in distress. She got up, opened cupboards and drawers, looked in the bathroom. No sign of a cat. Still troubled, she went back to bed, only to be wakened by the same sound. But this time she clearly saw Per's face. More than that, she then saw him stretched out full length, eyes glazed, his flanks, damp with perspiration, heaving.

Overwhelmed with foreboding, she cancelled her outing and returned to Malmö with all speed—first by aeroplane, then car. As she approached the house, she saw her host digging a hole under an apple tree. Taken aback, and seemingly embarrassed, he called to his wife, who came hurriedly, her eyes red with weeping, followed by the little boy Sven, who was sobbing.

Per had died the previous night.

Neighbours carved a tombstone under the apple-tree: for Per had been a wonderful cat—intelligent, affectionate, amusing—with a repertoire of tricks which he performed to the particular delight of Sven.

This happened many years ago. Sven is married now, and the father of three children whom he has brought up to be gentle and loving to cats.

A twelve-year-old child, on holiday in Cornwall in the summer of 1929, was sleeping in the same room as her mother and a younger brother when she woke in the night in a state of deep distress.

She told her mother that she had seen—framed, as it were, in the window—not the Cornish scene but, in the moonlit garden of the house next door but one to her home in London, her cat, to whom she was devoted, lying dead on the lawn.

Her distress was heightened by exasperation with her bewildered mother: 'Can't you *see*?' she cried desperately. Trying to reassure the child, the mother said there was nothing to see, nothing to fear—it was only a dream.

Eventually the child fell asleep, and in the morning no more was said. The mother, however, in writing to her husband, told him what had occurred, saying she was thankful that all was now well.

But all was *not* well. In reply her husband wrote that the cat had indeed been found dead on the lawn of the house next door but one —on the morning following the night during which the child had 'seen' her pet.

This story was told me by the 'child', a lady now living in Dulwich, and verified by her brother.

One day when I was a small child in Ireland my parents took me with them to a croquet party given by three old sisters who lived in a shabby yet imposing Georgian house.

I was watching the big coloured balls rolling over the lawn when I became aware of a silky white cat with a bushy tail walking across the grass. I ran towards him, hands outstretched to stroke him, but, although I could still see the cat, there was nothing to stroke, nothing to touch. For a moment he was transparent, then gone. 'A fairy cat,' I said to myself; and because I believed in fairies, the thought did not trouble me.

At tea I announced: 'I saw a fairy cat—there, on the lawn!' The face of the eldest sister grew pale, her expression anxious. I sensed that my remark, for some reason I could not understand, had not gone down well.

On the way home in the pony-trap I insisted: 'But I *did* see a fairy cat!' 'Not a fairy cat,' my father said quietly, 'a *phantom* cat.' I wondered what 'phantom' meant, but felt the subject had been closed.

Several persons, I was assured later, had seen this same cat from time to time, but how he came to be there was not disclosed. I only know that he was beautiful—nothing sinister about him.

Lord Barclay de Tolly tells how, in 1942, his mother was bombed out of her home. Being on leave at the time he took for the two of them an unfurnished ground-floor flat in a Victorian house in Station Road, Westgate. The sitting-room was fairly large: it had three doors, one opening into the hall, two into other rooms.

A few days after moving in, he was sitting listening to the radio—it was afternoon, and still broad daylight—when he was aware that there was a large tabby cat in the room. A bit puzzled, because the doors were shut, he told himself that the animal must have sneaked in earlier. And so he stood up and reached out a hand, when suddenly he realised that there was nothing to stroke—the cat had vanished! He was somewhat startled.

On a number of occasions the cat appeared again. He certainly looked solid, but when he walked up to one of the closed doors he disappeared. Lord Barclay wondered if this experience was purely subjective, until a former school friend of his remarked: 'I didn't know you had a cat.'

One day he called on an old lady living in the flat above. When he enquired if there was anything odd about the house, she replied: 'Oh, you mean the cat? He's always popping up all over the place!' Lots of visitors, it turned out, had seen this cat. There was nothing uncanny about him, no astral mewings; to all appearances he was a solid, sensible cat who just came and went.

* * *

Cats frequently sense the approach of their death. Numerous are the cats who, when grievously ill, withdraw to some quiet spot to await their end.

In an overgrown garden in Wiltshire I came upon a small gravestone half hidden by brambles. On it were carved the words:

> Mark, the Cat came here
> To die alone.
> November 1911.

George Borrow, the most tender-hearted of men, could not bear, we read in his biography by Herbert Jenkins, to think about a cat who, he was convinced, had slipped away to die in solitude. He searched for the animal, found her in a hedgerow, took her home, watched over her and cared for her until she died.

Andrew Lang records a somewhat similar incident that had a happier ending. An old cat, Gyp, having suffered a stroke, lived on but was clearly in terror of death. Treated with every possible care, he recovered his health and spirits, as was proved one day when he was seen on the roof of an outhouse, eagerly devouring a cold boiled chicken clutched between his forepaws.

Hal Summers, in 'My Old Cat', writes of his pet, in life gentle, happy, sleek, purring, who could meet death only in a mood of defiance: he could not pretend that all was well. To read this poem is to recall Dylan Thomas's words to his dying father:

> Do not go gentle into that good night.
> Rage, rage against the dying of the light.

Sometimes death comes to a cat swiftly and mercifully, just as when, in the world of classical mythology, Apollo the archer aims an unswerving shaft from his bow.

Angel lived in the heart of the country, in Suffolk. He was a splendid cat, the colour of marmalade dipped in flour. Brought as a kitten from Portmeirion, where cats, so they tell me, are normally this colour, he was large and plump, his fur short and thick his intelligent eyes a lambent green.

He used to come in each morning by the kitchen window, jump on to the draining-board, then on to the floor where a saucer of milk was waiting for him. One morning he did not finish his milk. Without warning, he toppled over on to one side and lay motionless. Death had come gently to a gentle cat.

* * *

If the bond between ourselves and other creatures is as close as it is, no wonder that the death of a much loved pet awakes in us both grief and questioning.

Heartbroken at the death of his cat, his beloved 'pupil' the Kater Murr, Ernst Hoffman, philosopher and composer, asked only this of his friends: to respect his grief by their silence. Kater Murr, he told them, had departed for a better world, fallen asleep to wake to a happier life.

And this brings to my mind Neville Braybrooke's poem 'A Writer's Cat', about his cat Lucca Ega. Troubled in childhood by the problems posed by the death of a cat or a dog, Neville had found comfort, indeed inspiration, in Anatole France's *Penguin Island*, which tells of a council being held in heaven to decide whether penguins baptised by St Maël could be considered as having souls. The solution was found by St Catherine of Alexandria, as the poem recounts:

> The sea throws up fishes and ideas;
> Two children dressed as penguins walk by its edge in
>   a carnival parade.
> I remember the day a favourite cat died.
> At dawn I carried him into the garden and laid him
>   on a bed of mint,
> Still breathing.
> The eyes I had known for almost thirteen years
>   followed me about.
> When the post arrived, he gave a short purr:
>
> It had been his habit since a kitten.
> It was his last link with my world of manuscripts
>   and books.
> Our parting would be soon.
>
> Later when I wrapped him in an old cardigan
> I thought of Anatole France and St Maël's baptism of
>   the penguins
> And how St Catherine had said:
> 'Give them souls—but tiny ones.'
>
> I will settle for that
> For my cat.

There is comfort in these lines. But comfort, though it mellows grief, does not wash it away. The pathos surrounding the death of a cat, this brief life enfolded in a sleep, speaks to us of the transience of all things.

For some years I used to watch from the window of a flat in London the two cats, one black, one sandy, belonging to Ralph Truman, the actor, and his wife. First one cat died, then the other. I would speak of them occasionally to Mr and Mrs Truman, but with restraint, not wanting to intensify their sorrow. Then one day, later on, I said: 'I still miss your cats.' Mrs Truman replied: 'I know . . . It's just that much less of love.'

* * *

Outside a blizzard was blowing; the wind shrilled. Inside, the invalid was sitting in the lamp-lit, oak-panelled hall, her big tabby cat on her lap. She was waiting to say goodbye to a clerical visitor, a canon lawyer, whom her host was going to accompany to the station. The cat sat up straight, an expectant look in his wide-open yellow eyes.

For months he had been a good cat. He had gone to bed each night between ten and eleven o'clock, curled up on the electric blanket on his mistress's bed, and slept until morning. Then, suddenly, things began to go wrong. He took to waking at 3 am, mewing to be let out of doors, then, after a while, howling to be let in. Night after night his mistress had to go down a flight of stairs to let him out, and then again to let him in. She was not fit for this. She might fall or have a heart attack . . .

As she sat there in the hall her host and their friend came down. Having bade her goodbye the canon lawyer, who had been troubled, on the invalid's account, by her pet's change of routine, suddenly turned round and, making the sign of the Cross, blessed the cat, using a blessing he had composed in the tradition of prayers contained in the *Rituale Romanum*:

> Benedictio Dei omnipotentis Patris et Filii et Spiritus Sancti, qui te tam pulchrum creavit, te semper bonum et mansuetum conservet et tandem locum in suo caelesti regno tibi inveniat. Amen.

> May the blessing of God Almighty, the Father, the Son and the Holy Spirit, who made you so beautiful a creature, keep you always good and gentle, and, at the last, find for you a place in His heavenly kingdom. Amen.

The two men went out into the blizzard. Wearing their black great-coats and fur hats, they looked like a couple of Russian princes. The snowflakes, in the light from the hall, fell like a golden shower; the interior of the car, lit up, made a golden canopy in the darkness of the night.

Many months have passed and not once, since then, has the cat disturbed his owner. He has slept on her bed each night, until seven o'clock in the morning.

Explain this as you will.

. . . *locum in suo caelesti regno :* the phrase echoes the neighbourly spirit that exists between men and animals in the Bible. Thomastic philosophy overweighted by Hellenic rationalism—the emphasis being on the reason and intellect—has in part been responsible for a lack of respect for the animal creation. In the early Church it was not so: centuries before St Francis of Assisi, Christians showed concern for animals. There are plenty of examples among the Desert Fathers, the Celtic scholars and the saints.

Again, St Chrysostom said we should be kind and gentle to animals for many reasons, but most of all because they are the same in origin as ourselves.

Sulpicius Severus, barrister to Petronius, said that every dumb beast was eloquent in Christ. If God created man he also created the animals: 'The animals of the forest are mine.'

Christ entered Jerusalem riding on an ass. He cared about the fall of a sparrow, and in the wilderness, he spent forty days in the company of the wild animals—not, as some would have us believe, as a penance, but, as the late Biblical scholar William Barclay emphasised, that the Creator might share in the life of his creatures.

St Paul stresses that the redemption applies to all of creation, not mankind alone.

* * *

There is a saying, attributed by some to Muhammad but believed by others to be Celtic in origin, to the effect that cats 'keep watch over us'.

Throughout a long life the old lady had been devoted to cats: her own cats, those belonging to friends and relations, and, perhaps most of all, unloved, unwanted strays. But that was all over now. She was dying. Her breathing was difficult, her strength waning; her hands moved restlessly over the fold of her sheet.

Suddenly her faded eyes lit up. She tried to reach out her arms. Her faltering words were coherent: 'The cats! All those beautiful cats! Do you see the cats?'

And she sank back on her pillows . . .

A prayer in the Roman liturgy asks that angels may receive the dying and welcome them into paradise: *deducant angeli in paradisium*. Angels are pure spirit; but they are able, theologians tell us, when sent as messengers into time from eternity, to assume a corporeal form.

It was late evening. The blocks of high-rise flats reached up into the gathering autumn gloom, lighted windows forming horizontal bars of gold.

The priest, warmly welcomed by a family living on the eleventh floor, unpacked what, since the days of Flanders in World War I, has been known as a 'Mass kit'. He was shown into a room empty except for a table which was to serve as an altar. No one, since the family had moved into the flat—neither members of the family nor anyone else—had been able to sleep in this room so cold was it. It was not a normal cold that could be tempered by a radiator or a heater. No, it was a sinister, unnerving cold that paralysed mind and body alike. That was why Mass was to be offered—with the intention that the evil influence would once and for all be dispelled.

The Mass proceeded. The candle flames burned steadily on the altar. The murmur of prayer led up to the Consecration. Then, in the silence preceding and following the raising of the Host and the chalice, suddenly there rang out the voices of cats: a great swelling chorus, its volume increased, it seemed, by voices of yet more cats from far away—mysterious, triumphant, proclaiming and rejoicing in the victory of good over evil.

Then, again, silence.

The family looked at one another. The Mass moved quietly to its close.

As the son of the house, accompanied by his young bride, was seeing the priest off, 'Father,' he said, 'did you hear all those cats?'

The priest nodded. 'I'd no idea', the young man continued, 'there were so many cats around here.'

This happened many months ago, since when the priest has kept in touch with the family and visited the flat. A number of persons have slept peacefully in the room, both members of the family and others. No complaints, no mention of the cold. Indeed, it is a favourite room.

But the chorus of cats is not forgotten. Once again recently the son mentioned to the priest his surprise at there being so many cats in the neighbourhood that evening. His young wife, who had been laughing, suddenly became serious. 'Father,' she said—and her voice was quiet—'there *are* no cats around here!'

* * *

Respect the cat, I beg you, for he is unique. Respect him, for he is deserving of respect. Respect his lineage lost in obscurity, his

'Respect his lineage lost in obscurity, his Egyptian ancestry, the reverence accorded him in temples of the East.'

Egyptian ancestry, the reverence accorded him in temples of the East. Respect him for his grace and elegance, his soundless movements, his waving tail, his composure, self-assurance, independence, eyes deep as a pool or lustrous as jewels. Respect him for the services he renders, for killing rodents, snakes, wasps and flies. For keeping us company, playing with our children, making us laugh.

Respect the cat for the place he occupies in the animal kingdom. Consider the conclusion drawn by Mivart, that on the physical level the cat rather than man is the best fitted among mammals to make his way in the world. Respect him as God's creature; the Lord, St John of the Cross reminds us, bestowed upon all things touches of himself: 'The creatures are traces of God's passing, wherein he reveals his might, power and wisdom.'

Respect the intelligence of the cat. Respect his discernment. A dog and a cat, Russian legend tells, were posted as sentinels at the gate of Paradise. The Evil One tried to sneak in, disguised as a mouse. The dog let him pass. The cat pounced and slew him.

Priére du chat

O mon maître,
Ne me prends pas pour esclave, car j'ai en moi le goût
de la liberté.
Ne cherche pas à deviner mes secrets, car j'ai en moi le
goût du mystère.
Ne me contrains pas aux caresses, car j'ai en moi le
gôut de la pudeur.
Ne m'humilie pas, car j'ai en moi le goût de la fierté.
Ne m'abandonne pas, car j'ai en moi le goût de la
fidélité.
Sache m'aimer et je saurai t'aimer, car j'ai en moi le
goût de l'amitié.

The cat's prayer

O my Master,
Do not expect me to be your slave, I have a thirst for
freedom.
Do not probe my secret thoughts, I have a love of
mystery.
Do not smother me with caresses, I have a preference
for reserve.
Do not humiliate me, I have a sense of pride.
Do not, I beg, abandon me, I have a sure fidelity.
I'll return your love for me, I have a sense of true
devotion.

Belgian traditional

Select bibliography

The following is a selection from the books that meant most in writing *In Celebration of Cats*.

Aberconway, Christabel, Lady, *A Dictionary of Cat Lovers* (Michael Joseph, 1949; reprinted 1968)

Baudelaire, Charles, *Les Fleurs du Mal* (first published 1857; Blackwell, 1966)

Beadle, Muriel, *The Cat* (Collins, 1977)

Budge, Sir E. A. Wallis, *The Gods of the Egyptians* (Methuen, 1902)

Bulgakov, Mikhail (trans Michael Glenny), *Master and Margarita* (Collins, 1967)

Carr, Samuel, *Poetry of Cats* (Batsford, 1974)

Champfleury, *Les Chats* (1870)

Clark, S. R. L., *The Moral Status of Animals* (OUP, 1977)

Colette (trans Antonia White), *The Cat* (Secker & Warburg, 1953; reprinted 1971)

—— (trans Enid McLeod), *Creatures Great and Small* (Secker & Warburg, 1951)

Dale-Green, Patricia, *Cult of the Cat* (Heinemann, 1963)

Dudley, Ernest, *Scrap* (Muller, 1974; Coronet, 1977)

Eliot, T. S., *Old Possum's Book of Practical Cats* (Faber, 1939; new ed 1975)

Fox, Michael, *Understanding your Cat* (Bantam, 1977)

Gallico, Paul, *Jennie* (Michael Joseph, 1950; Penguin, 1970)

—— *Thomasina* (Michael Joseph, 1957)

Gay, John, *John Gay's Book of Cats* (David & Charles, 1975)

Gielgud, Val, *My Cats and Myself* (Michael Joseph, 1972)

Gineste, Raoul, *Chattes et Chats* (1892)

Hudson, W. H., *The Book of a Naturalist* (Hodder & Stoughton, 1919)

Joseph, Michael, *Charles: The Story of a Friendship* (Michael Joseph, 1943)

Kirk, Mildred, *The Everlasting Cat* (Faber, 1978)

Lane, Charles, *Rabbits, Cats and Cavies* (Dent, 1903)

Lee, Elizabeth, *A Quorum of Cats* (Elek, 1976)

Mivart, St George, *The Cat* (Murray, 1881)

Montgomery, John, *Arthur, the Television Cat* (W. H. Allen, 1975)

Necker, Claire, *The Natural History of Cats* (Barnes, NY, 1971)

Oldfield, H. M., *The Cat in the Mysteries of Religion and Magic* (Rider, 1930)

Penguin Book of Animal Verse (ed Macbeth, 1965)

Pond, Grace, *The Observer's Book of Cats* (Warne, 1968)

Raleigh, Scott, Elizabeth and Oliphant Jackson, *Practical Guide to Cats* (Hamlyn, 1976)

Rowse, A. L., *Peter, the White Cat of Trenarren* (Michael Joseph, 1974)

Seraphim, Sister, *All God's Creatures* (Dodd, Mead, NY, 1966)

Sillar, F. C., and Ruth Meyler, *Cats Ancient and Modern* (White Lion, 1976)

Stuart, Dorothy, *Book of Cats, Literary, Legendary and Historical* (Methuen, 1959)

Tangye, Derek, *A Cat in the Window* (Michael Joseph, 1962)

Topsell, Edward, *The Historie of Foure-Footed Beastes* (1607, reprinted Frank Cass, 1967)

Uzé, Marcel (trans Helen Slonim), *The Cat in Nature, History and Art* (Hyperon, Milan, nd)

Vechten, Carl Van, *The Tiger in the House* (Jonathan Cape, 1938)

Warner, Charles Dudley, *My Summer in a Garden* (Hutchinson, 1871)

White, Gilbert, *The Natural History of Selborne* (1789; reprinted Dent, 1971; Penguin, 1977)

Wodehouse, P. G., *The Catnappers* (formerly *Aunts Aren't Gentlemen*, Barrie & Jenkins, 1974)